Syria and Iran

CHATHAM HOUSE PAPERS

A Middle East Programme Publication
Programme Director: Rosemary Hollis

The Royal Institute of International Affairs, at Chatham House in London, has provided an impartial forum for discussion and debate on current international issues for 75 years. Its resident research fellows, specialized information resources, and range of publications, conferences, and meetings span the fields of international politics, economics, and security. The Institute is independent of government.

Chatham House Papers are short monographs on current policy problems which have been commissioned by the RIIA. In preparing the papers, authors are advised by a study group of experts convened by the RIIA, and publication of a paper indicates that the Institute regards it as an authoritative contribution to the public debate. The Institute does not, however, hold opinions of its own; the views expressed in this publication are the responsibility of the authors.

CHATHAM HOUSE PAPERS

Syria and Iran

Rivalry and Cooperation

Hussein J. Agha and

Ahmad S. Khalidi

PINTER
PUBLISHERS
London

THE ROYAL INSTITUTE
OF INTERNATIONAL
AFFAIRS

Pinter
A Cassell Imprint
Wellington House, 125 Strand, London WC2R 0BB, United Kingdom

First published in 1995

British Library Cataloguing in Publication Data
A CIP catalogue record for this book is available from the British Library

ISBN 1-85567-235-9 (Paperback)
     1-85567-234-0 (Hardback)

Typeset by Koinonia Limited
Printed and bound in Great Britain by
Biddles Limited, Guildford and King's Lynn

Contents

Contents

Foreword

There can be few issues even in the normally opaque art of Middle East politics which are as impenetrable as the Iranian–Syrian axis. Yet this relationship has now lasted for more than fifteen years. It has, in short, proved much more enduring than most interstate ties in a region notorious for its convulsions and discontinuities. The enduring nature of this relationship is even more surprising if one bears in mind the alacrity with which Middle East experts have blithely predicted its imminent demise over the past decade and a half.

One need look no further for these routine errors of judgment than the paucity of serious investigations of Iranian–Syrian relations. Why this has been the case is indeed difficult to fathom. One can only assume that it is because the relationship was deemed too impenetrable that scholars and analysts have shied away from it. Needless to say, this has been the worst possible reason for ignoring the subject. Mindful of the need to illuminate issues which have remained in shadow, the Middle East Programme at Chatham House was eager to undertake a serious study of the subject. We were pleased to be able to commission two of the leading policy commentators on contemporary Middle East affairs, Hussein Agha and Ahmad Khalidi, to undertake this work.

In the first book to be published on the issue, Agha and Khalidi have produced a work of great authority and great subtlety. They have fully researched the origins of the relationship and the course of its evolution. In so doing, their contribution to an understanding of the dynamics of Middle East politics goes well beyond the purely bilateral relationship between Damascus and Tehran. In accordance with their brief, the authors have also considered the impact which the axis has had and may yet have on the Arab–Israeli dispute. Their important and welcome conclusion is that Syria's Iranian connection will not impede the fortunes of peace-making. Indeed, they argue that it is because the preoccupations of the one party are largely peripheral to the central strategic concerns of the other that the axis has proved remarkably enduring. In the light of such a view, it is therefore likely that the Iranian–Syrian relationship will endure. With this book, we can now all understand why.

May 1995   Dr Philip Robins
                                            St Antony's College, Oxford

Acknowledgments

We have benefited from intensive unattributable discussions with many Syrian, Iranian, Palestinian, Lebanese and other officials and private individuals who were generous with their time, knowledge and experience.

We are grateful to the United States Institute of Peace in Washington, DC and the W. Alton Jones Foundation in Charlottesville, VA for sponsoring this study. We are indebted to Ambassador Samuel Lewis and Dr George Perkovitch for their pivotal role in supporting and encouraging this project.

We should like to thank the Royal Institute of International Affairs (Chatham House) in London for providing a home for the project. Particular thanks go to Dr Philip Robins, former Head of the Middle East Programme, for his clear direction and constructive comments, Sir John Moberly for his interest and advice, Jill Devey for her logistical help and support, Gillian Bromley for her editorial skills, Margaret May and Hannah Doe in the Publications Department, and Dr Rosemary Hollis, Head of the Middle East Programme, for seeing the project through to fruition.

Jubin Goodarzi provided us with exemplary research assistance and Christin Marschall with food for thought from her own research.

On a more personal note, special thanks go to Mohsen and the family, Ana Drummond, and Marion and the Khalidi kids – to all of whom we owe gratitude for their support while this work was in progress.

May 1995   H.J.A.
                                                                          A.S.K.

Abbreviations

GCC	Gulf Cooperation Council
MTCR	Missile Technology Control Regime
PDRY	People's Democratic Republic of Yemen
PFLP	Popular Front for the Liberation of Palestine
PFLP-GC	Popular Front for the Liberation of Palestine (General Command)
PDFLP	Popular Democratic Front for the Liberation of Palestine (later PDF – Popular Democratic Front)
PKK	Kurdish Workers Party
PLO	Palestine Liberation Organization
PNA	Palestine National Authority
PNC	Palestine National Council
PUK	Patriotic Union of Kurdistan
SLA	South Lebanon Army

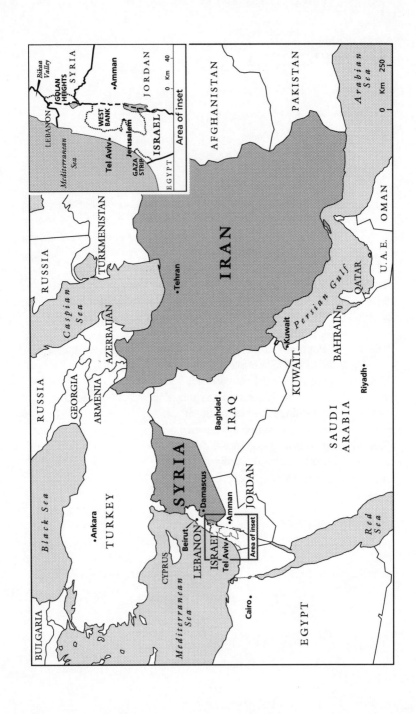

Chapter 1

The roots of the Syrian–
Iranian alliance

The Syrian–Iranian alliance has evolved over time. While some of the initial impulses behind the alliance seem to have faded, other factors have come to the fore as developments both within the two countries and across their range of interests continue to affect the scope and nature of their relationship. A few factors may be seen to stand out as permanent features and possible determinants of this alliance and its future direction – primary among them the common interest in Iraq and the vital role of the Shia community in Lebanon for Syria and Iran alike – but the underlying causes for what is superficially an unlikely relationship go somewhat deeper. Beneath considerations relating to the regional balance of power and the preservation of political and other interests lies a web of historical, socio-cultural and geopolitical factors that have helped to shape the alliance and sustain it over much of the past decade and a half. Indeed, in an area of unstable and fluctuating alliances, the Syrian–Iranian relationship has proved to be more constant and durable than almost any other in the region.

Syrian interest in Iran and Iranian interest in Syria and Lebanon predate the fall of the Shah and the current close relations between Baathist Syria and the Islamic Republic of Iran. Socio-religious ties between Jabal Amil (the Lebanese Shiites' historical home in South Lebanon) and Safavid Iran (the Shiite Persian dynasty) can be traced back to the sixteenth century, and an extensive network of familial and commercial ties still underpins the political intercourse between the various sects and groupings in the area. The more recent Syrian–Iranian antagonisms of the 1950s and 1960s were largely a result of Imperial Iranian concern about the radical nature of pan-Arab nationalism and its potentially destabilizing effect, both in the region at large and within the Arabic-speaking

1

areas of Iran itself. Equally, the prevalent view among the Arab nationalist regimes of Egypt, Iraq and Syria was that Iran under the Shah was but one element of a grand strategic design – including Israel – engineered by the West to contain and defeat the surge towards Arab unity. In so far as the Shah represented a revived Persian nationalism, and given the history of Arab–Persian antagonism, Arab nationalist aspirations thus appeared in natural opposition to both the symbols and the policies of Imperial Iran.

By the mid-1970s a number of new factors were beginning to have a substantial effect on Arab–Iranian relations generally and on Syria's attitude towards Iran in particular. The relative retreat of pan-Arab nationalism after the death of Nasser and the consolidation of the mutually inimical Baathist regimes in Syria and Iraq opened the door for a new triangular configuration. Syrian interest in Iran appears to have shifted away from a purely ideological animus towards a more calculating rationale based on considerations of power and balance, with the competing regime in Iraq on the one hand and in broader regional terms on the other. Iran's role in constraining Iraqi freedom of action and as a possible counterweight against other Arab parties, including Egypt, may have added to Syria's incentives for rethinking its posture towards Iran. This process was matched by a similar evolution in Iranian policies, from a posture of at least public reticence in the Arab–Israeli conflict (while conducting a purposeful but low-profile collaboration with Israel) to a more forward 'pro-Arab' line in the 1973 war, including the offer of economic and medical aid to Syria. Aware of the developing links between Islamic revolutionary elements and the Palestinian and militant Shia groups in Lebanon, Iran may have sought to strengthen its ties with Syria as a potential means of counter-pressure against its internal opposition. At the same time, more confident of its own economic and military strength, Iran was reaching out to various Arab interlocutors as a means of expanding its regional role and presence. By late 1975 it had built up a new working relationship with Syria, exemplified by the 1974 economic agreement between the two countries and President Assad's official visit to Tehran in December 1975 (not to be repeated until September 1990), and had also signed the Algiers accord on the Shatt al-Arab waterway, thus neatly balancing its opening to Syria with a parallel opening to Iraq, both executed within a general framework of improved ties with other major Arab actors, particularly Sadat's Egypt.

Although the detente of the mid-1970s between Syria and Imperial Iran had no lasting effect either on their bilateral relations or on the regional balance at large, Syria's perceptions of Iran as a balancing force against Iraq – and vice versa – may have taken root around this time. The modern geopolitics of Syrian–Iraqi relations on the one hand and Iranian–Iraqi relations on the other, rather than any regime-specific motivation or function, thus appear to form one of the cornerstones of Syrian–Iranian relations; but cutting across and merging into the geopolitical aspect are many other factors deeply embedded in the sociopolitical, sectarian and religious fabric of the area.

Lebanon and the Shia–Alawite connection

Since coming to power in 1963 the Syrian Baath party had been aware of the regime's narrow sectarian base. In 1971 the Alawite Hafiz al-Assad was elected as the first non-Sunni President of Syria. Historically maligned as heretics by Sunnis and Shia alike, the Syrian Alawites had long sought a precarious balance between obtaining recognition of their self-proclaimed status as a branch of *Ithna-ashari* (Twelver) Shiism and the preservation of their own ethno-cultural identity and arcane beliefs. But besides the sectarian import of the new leader's allegiance, the *political* role of the Alawis as the power base for the Syrian Baath helped to accentuate the problem of Alawi legitimization and add to the importance of the Shia dimension of Syrian policy, and hence of relations with the Shiites of Lebanon and Iran respectively.

The development of Syrian policy towards the Shia of Lebanon and Iran was also bound up with the separate development of Lebanese Shia politics and, naturally, with developments within Iran. The new political self-assertion of the Shia in the Lebanon since the late 1960s was accompanied by a keen awareness on the part of both the Syrian and the local Lebanese Shiite leaders of their mutual interests and common cause. For the Lebanese Shia, the Alawite search for legitimacy ran parallel to the Shiite need for a powerful and reliable external ally. This relationship was bolstered from time to time by close personal ties between the leaders of both parties, as exemplified by the relationship between Assad and the Iranian-Lebanese Shiite leader Musa as-Sadr in the early 1970s. Sadr, born in Qom and educated at Najjaf and al-Azhar in Cairo, had established himself in Lebanon in 1959, and soon emerged as the most authoritative spokesman for the Lebanese Shiite community. Sadr's *fatwa* regarding local Lebanese Alawites as Shiites in July 1973, although of dubious ecumenical value (especially given that the Alawites subsequently reasserted their separate religious identity), can be seen as a simultaneously personal and highly political gesture towards Assad himself. This gesture meshed neatly with Sadr's goal of maintaining strong ties with Syria as a powerful counterweight to the other parties in the Lebanese cauldron, and was important too in the context of Syria's own interest in the ever-growing and increasingly radicalized Lebanese Shiite community. The relative stabilization of Syrian–Iranian relations in the mid-1970s accordingly did not preclude the development of close ties between Damascus and a number of leading figures in the Iranian opposition. With Sadr, by now a personal friend of Assad, acting as one of the principal go-betweens, major Iranian opposition figures were accorded special privileges and protection by the Syrian authorities. When Ayatollah Khomeini was evicted from Iraq in October 1978, Assad offered to receive the Iranian leader in Damascus first – an offer gracefully declined at the time but still appreciated by Khomeini, as was conveyed to Syrian officials some years later. Nevertheless, the role of the various personalities involved and of the legitimization issue in forming and furthering links between the Syrian regime and the Shia of Lebanon and Iran should not be overstated. While Syrian Sunnis were unlikely to have been mollified by Shiite recognition of the Alawis in any case, the political import of the legitimization issue has receded as relations between the Alawite minority and the Sunni majority appear to have stabilized in recent years. However, the Shiite–Alawite connection did play an important role in the development of Syrian–Iranian relations and may in fact be seen as one of the main motors of the emerging alliance between the two countries. This connection has also helped to establish Lebanon as an important point of intersection between the socio-religious element of Shiite–Alawite relations and the regional and strategic interests of both Syria and Iran.

Developments in Lebanon have guaranteed the Shiites a significant role in the formulation of Syria's policy in the area. The growing presence of the PLO in Lebanon since 1969, accelerated by its eviction from Jordan in 1970, saw the country undergoing two simultaneous processes of transformation. First, it was slowly but surely turning into a major theatre of military operations between Israel and the Palestinians, with the constant prospect of spiralling violence that could precipitate a Syrian–Israeli confrontation; and concurrently, partly as a result of the pressures generated by the Israeli–Palestinian conflict, the authority and integrity of the Lebanese state was coming under severe strain, creating a potentially dangerous power vacuum on Syria's immediate flank. As Lebanon slid into progressive dissolution, the local dimensions of the conflict became inextricably intertwined with the external, and Syria's concerns about the implications of a wholesale Palestinian–Israeli confrontation became virtually inseparable from its concerns that hostile outside parties, ranging from the United States to Egypt to Iraq, might find common cause with local Lebanese or Palestinian proxies to pose a direct challenge to Syria itself or to establish a new Lebanon free from Syria's influence. From this viewpoint, the value of the Lebanese Shia as a reliable political and military ally to Syria within the Muslim camp cannot be overestimated, especially against the background of the growing rift between Syria and the Palestinian left-Muslim alliance in the crucial first years of the Lebanese civil war.

Lebanon and the Iranian–Palestinian connection

Alongside the growing importance of Lebanon for Syria ran the development of a new set of ties between the then underground opposition to the Shah in Iran and the Palestinian movement, which had become firmly ensconced as a semi-autonomous actor in Lebanon by the early 1970s. The first contacts between the two groups occurred as early as 1968, after the battle of Karameh in the Jordan Valley had seemed to portend the birth of a new and vitally charged revolutionary movement in the area. Initially Palestinian–Iranian contacts centred on the leftist-Marxist Iranian opposition groups, but these were rapidly augmented by a direct line between the Palestinian mainstream movement Fateh and Khomeini's clerical opposition. In late 1968, in a curiously parallel move to Sadr's 1973 *fatwa* regarding the Alawites of Lebanon, Khomeini himself issued a similar *fatwa* supporting Fateh's call for armed struggle against Israel and authorizing Iranian payments to the 'Palestinian Fedaiyun' as part of the holy Muslim obligation to *Zakat* (the percentage of a Muslim's income that is devoted to charity). By 1969–70 various Iranian opposition groups, including the Mojaheddin Khalq and the Fedayeen Khalq, had been trained by Fateh, the PFLP (Popular Front for the Liberation of Palestine), and the PDFLP (Popular Democratic Front for the Liberation of Palestine) in Palestinian camps in Jordan as well as in Lebanon and Iraq. During 1969 the special ties between Fateh and the Islamic opposition groups were expanded by Iranian field visits to Fateh bases in South Lebanon, engineered on the Iranian side largely by Muhammed Saleh al-Husseini, a confidant of the then Iraqi-based Khomeini, and including senior Iranian clerics such Sheikh Hassan Karoubi, Jallaleddin Farisi and Abbas Madani. This led to the development of close personal relations between key figures on both sides. The eventual list of Iranian revolutionary graduates from Fateh camps in Lebanon and elsewhere was impressive and spanned virtually the whole of the first rank of Iranian officials to take power after the fall of the Shah. The Iranian experience with the Palestinians in Lebanon was important on more than one level. First, it helped to consolidate the ideological antipathy of the Iranian revolution towards Israel that already existed as a result of the perceived alliance between Israel and the Shah. (The fact that this antipathy has apparently outlived the ideological opposition of Fateh itself to a political settlement with Israel may indicate – among other things – the continuing resonance of the Lebanese experience for at least some elements among the ruling elite in Tehran.) On a more operational level, it also demonstrated Lebanon's potential as a point of access to the wider regional arena, later exploited in the despatch of Revolutionary Guards to the Bikaa in 1982 and the subsequent active pursuit of revolutionary policies via proxies in Lebanon.

The Iranian experience with the Palestinians is just one element in the interaction between Syria, the Shia and Iran in Lebanon. While Fateh was assiduously cultivating its relations with the Iranian revolutionary movement, it had already built up a significant but progressively souring relationship with the local Shia. Well before Sadr emerged as the major Muslim ally of Syria in Lebanon, the Palestinians had been instrumental in establishing and supporting the newly awakened Lebanese Shia political movement, not least by their initial direct contact with the Shia popular base in South Lebanon and elsewhere. The Lebanese Shiite movement Amal (formally established by Sadr in 1974) was from its inception not only modelled on Fateh but armed, trained and staffed by both Lebanese and Palestinan cadres of the Palestinian movement in an attempt to create a symbiotic relationship between the oppressed Lebanese of the South and the dispossessed Palestinians who lived among them. Israel's escalating military response to the Palestinian build-up in South Lebanon and elsewhere at first seemed to create the right environment for such a symbiosis. Between the Cairo agreement of 1969 (which granted them the right to operate in South Lebanon) and the mid-1970s, the Palestinians helped to galvanize the development of political Shiism in Lebanon and accelerate its social and political demands by weakening the central Lebanese authority and thus giving the Shia greater freedom to organize and consolidate their own political movement. Not surprisingly, however, this relationship began to face increasing stress as Israeli reprisals raised the cost of the Palestinian struggle in South Lebanon and Shia resentment at the sometimes high-handed methods of the Palestinians started to mount. The local Shiite interest in closer ties with Syria that had crystallized by the outbreak of the Lebanese civil war in 1975 can thus be seen to reflect at least partly a loss of faith in the PLO as mentor and model (though not necessarily a loss of faith in the Palestinian 'cause' itself) almost at the same time that the revolutionary Iranian movement's ties with the PLO were reaching their height. It was this germinating antagonism between substantial elements among the Lebanese Shia and the Palestinians that was later to create an awkward split between the pro-Iranian and pro-Syrian trends within the Shia community itself, and bring new tension to the alliance between Syria and Iran.

The Shiite religious schools

During the period before the Iranian revolution, revolutionary Islamic notions of government were being developed and elaborated among the forces opposed to the Shah in a remarkable process of pan-Shiite cross-fertilization. The religious schools of Qom in Iran and Najjaf in Iraq (particularly the latter) acted as a magnet and meeting-point for Shiite scholars and divines from Iran, Lebanon and Iraq, where the foundations were laid for similar – though not always identical – world-views and a network of personal friendships and politico-religious allegiances that were to have a significant impact on the region as a whole. Among the Lebanese Shia clergy who emerged from this network were Musa Sadr himself, Muhammed Mahdi Shamseddin (later Sadr's deputy and putative successor) and Mohammed Hussein Fadlallah (later to become 'spiritual leader' of Hizbullah in Lebanon). Other scholar-activists included Baqir as-Sadr, who went on to form Ad-Dawwa in Iraq, the precursor of other Shiite and Islamic movements in the area. Through his tenure in Najjaf between 1965 and 1978, Ayatollah Khomeini and his Iran-based colleagues were at the centre of this intellectual and political cauldron. The relationship between Sadr and other Lebanese Shia clergy and Khomeini helped to establish the ties that were subsequently to facilitate revolutionary Iran's entry into the Lebanese arena. Although his political and religious credentials were not unchallenged either inside or outside Iran, Khomeini was eventually to provide the single most important inspiration for Islamic activism, Shia and Sunni alike. In a sense Khomeini's Islamic vision was both eclectic and ecumenical: although deeply embedded in an Iranian/Shiite conception of Islam, it nonetheless carefully carried a transnational and trans-sectarian appeal. Despite the peculiarly Shiite nature of the Najjaf convocations, these gatherings may thus have helped to soften the new revolutionary dog-ma's narrow sectarian edge. The comparatively mixed experience of Najjaf and the interaction between Arab and Persian scholars and clergy may have also facilitated revolutionary Iran's non-sectarian and non-nationalist approach to its relations with Syria and its role in Lebanon, and vice versa.

Chapter 2

Critical stages in the evolution of the alliance

Syria and the Iranian revolution

The fall of the Shah in January 1979 seemed to pave the way for a new strategic alignment that would bring together Syria, Iran, the PLO and other 'radical' parties in the area such as Libya and South Yemen. For the Syrians, the Iranian revolution could hardly have been more timely: Syria's sense of growing isolation and strategic vulnerability had been heightened as a result of Egypt's defection from the struggle against Israel and the finalization of the Camp David Accords in March 1979. The failure of any real moves towards a Syrian–Iraqi rapprochement and the escalation of tension with Iraq after the alleged 'pro-Syrian' coup attempt in Iraq in July of that year put paid to the notion of any new Arab constellation that could redress the standing imbalance in power in Israel's favour. Syria was also concerned that Egypt – now firmly in the 'pro-Western' camp – would draw other key Arab parties in its wake, including Jordan, thus further increasing its isolation and weakening its position *vis-à-vis* Israel. Since the outbreak of the civil war in 1975 Syria's entanglement in Lebanon had created constant friction with the PLO and the Lebanese leftist alliance – Syria's ostensibly 'natural' partners – on the one hand, and had eventually led to deteriorating relations with Syria's former Christian right-wing allies on the other, both developments occurring against the ever-present threat of a possible massive Israeli intervention against Lebanon and Syria itself, already previewed in Israel's 1978 'Litani' incursion into South Lebanon. Internally, a growing Sunni fundamentalist movement led by the Ikhwan Muslimun (Muslim Brotherhood), aided and abetted by Iraq and Iraqi agents working via Lebanon, posed a grave internal threat to President

Assad's regime, challenging both its ability to maintain law and order and its very legitimacy. At a stroke, the Iranian revolution reshaped the regional balance against both Israel and Iraq, resurrected a powerful potential ally in place of Egypt, opened the door to Syrian–Iranian concordance in Lebanon, added to the muscle and credibility of the anti-Western/anti-US forces in the area and raised the prospects for some relief of some of the internal pressures on the Assad regime.

The revolution opened the door for a fundamentally new Iranian profile in the area. The power of true revolutionary Islam having been demonstrated, the possibility of forging a new regional order with Iran at its hub was not necessarily fanciful. The new regime in Tehran moved quickly to consolidate its relations with Syria and the PLO (with Arafat as the first foreign dignitary – and only Arab leader ever – to be received by Khomeini in Tehran), and its anti-Israeli stance appeared to provide the cement for this vital new axis. But the very emergence of a Shiite revolutionary power with great potential wealth and significant military power was destabilizing in regional terms. Traditional Iraqi fears of Persian expansionism were now compounded by a perceived internal secessionist threat from the Iraqi Shiite majority, encouraged by Iran and stimulated by its example. Added to this were the danger of an Iranian–Syrian axis that would effectively act as a giant geopolitical pincer against Iraq, and the challenge from an ideologically potent movement that had a more 'advanced' and credible commitment to the Palestinian cause than many of the Arab regimes themselves. The ensuing Iran–Iraq war was the result of a combination of historical rivalry, sectarian divisions, geopolitics and ideological challenge.

The Iran–Iraq war and the Iraqi factor

The Iraqi invasion of Iran in September 1980 helped to prepare the ground for a formal alliance between Syria and Iran. During the first phase of the war, between 1980 and 1982, a number of considerations appear to have been paramount. For the Iranians, the Syrians offered an indirect means of military pressure on Iraq and a direct source of arms for the beleaguered Iranian armed forces. The Iraqi command was reportedly forced to maintain deployment of a number of divisions on the Syrian border for both defensive and deterrent purposes. Syrian arms shipments sent with the apparent consent of the Soviet Union were particularly welcome given the Western embargo and the fact that some 70 per cent of Iranian equipment before the revolution was of Western origin. Syrian support for the Kurds and sponsorship of Talbani's Patriotic Union of Kurdistan (PUK), as well as of the combined Iraqi opposition National Progressive and Democratic Front, helped to keep up the pressure on Iraq's northern borders, tying down another not insignificant portion of Saddam Hussein's war machine.

Syria's political stance in support of Iran was also vital. Despite Saddam's best efforts, the Syrian position (and, to a lesser extent, the initial positions of the PLO and Libya as well) helped to prevent the war from turning into an all-out Persian–Arab confrontation or a straight Sunni–Shiite split across the region. Iran's own declarative stance on the Palestinian issue facilitated the Syrian argument that Iraq was destroying a potentially valuable ally of the Arabs rather than confronting a new non-Arab strategic threat. Nonetheless, Syria's active – or even tacit – alignment behind the pro-Iraq majority among the Arab states would have dealt a severe blow to Iran's access to the Arab world (particularly to its vital Shiite constituency in Lebanon) and could have weakened its already fragile military situation in the field. The maintenance of good relations with Syria afforded Iran another advantage, namely potential Syrian mediation with a number of other key states, specifically Saudi Arabia and the Gulf states. Although fearful of Iran's revolutionary vitality and its possible appeal to the sizeable Shiite minorities in the Gulf itself, the Gulf states were simultaneously uneasy about the prospects of a decisive Iraqi victory. Syria was thus ideally placed to play a bridging role with the Gulf, first on account of its supposed influence with Tehran, and second as a potential lever against Iraq. Internationally, Syria's close ties with the Soviet Union offered Iran an invaluable channel to the superpower most dangerously placed on Iran's immediate borders. Quite apart from Khomeinist ideological opposition to the Soviet Union and the new regime's eventual showdown with the Tudeh (Iranian communist) party, Iran was aware of the need to keep state-to-state relations with the Soviet Union on an even keel for any number of political, economic, ethno-sectarian and strategic reasons. Syria's good offices may also have occasionally helped to sharpen Soviet responsiveness to Iranian needs, as was apparently the case with regard to Soviet military trans-shipments to Iran via Syria.

For its part, Syria's pre-revolutionary ties with the Iranian leadership had begun to pay off. Most importantly, Iraq's invasion of Iran opened up the prospect of the eventual defeat and downfall of Saddam Hussein's regime. At worst the war portended a protracted and heavy Iraqi engagement in Iran that would deflect Iraqi attention away from Syria and allow the Assad regime greater margins of manouevre in the Mashriq (the old Levant) at large. Although the possibility of an Iranian defeat may have initially caused Syria some concern, it was evident after a few weeks of the war that a clear-cut victory for either side was not imminent. Syria's gains from Iraq's inability to score a decisive victory added up as the conflict turned into a war of attrition. Its newly discovered role as mediator gave Damascus a particular advantage with the Gulf states when soliciting economic and financial aid, and its relations with Iran carried a subtle undercurrent of threat to those who feared the prospect of an Iranian victory. At the same time Syria appeared as a potential counterweight to Iraq without the expansionist hegemonist tendencies that tinged Iraq's attitude to the Gulf – a balancing role that was later to stand it in good stead in the Gulf crisis of 1990–1.

The alliance with Iran also provided Syria with considerable backbone in the inter-Arab and Arab–Israeli arenas. Deserted by Egypt, Syria's long-standing quest for a viable multi-front strategy *vis-à-vis* Israel had for a moment appeared revivable. This time the formulation was not an extension southwards towards Egypt nor towards a traditional 'eastern front' configuration with Iraq, but rather northwards through the addition of extra strategic and military depth via Iran. Iraq's invasion of Iran immediately upset this grand scheme, causing Syria genuine anger and concern. But the Syrian position was not one of total loss; for, by pinning down Saddam, Iran left Syria free to concentrate its energies on facing Israel. Equally, Iran offered the prospect of some future strategic reassurance against Israel, albeit qualified by the outcome of the war with Iraq. In addition, Iran provided a supportive bulwark against Egyptian penetration of the Mashriq and a counterbalance against the gradually crystallizing Egypt-Jordan-Iraq-Saudi Arabia axis. Syria's interest in firming up its relationship with Iran may also have had a pre-emptive element: by getting there first, Syria could claim some priority in the face of possible competition. Initially, Syria may have even taken into account the need to prevent a possible Iranian backslide towards Israel – a possibility not totally incompatible with the perceived interests of some elements in the Iranian leadership, as later evidenced by the Iran–Contra affair.

The year 1982 was a turning-point in the Syrian–Iranian relationship. The extension of Israeli law to the Golan in November 1981 may have added extra impetus to the Syrian interest in sealing its alliance with Iran; also by late 1981 Iran appears to have decided to press for some form of formalization of its relationship with Syria. In early 1982 these efforts were galvanized by events in Syria when Assad faced his most difficult internal challenge yet, a steady bombing campaign mounted by the Iraqi-backed Ikhwan culminating in open rebellion in Hama in February. An escalation into all-out confessional conflict along Sunni–Alawite lines could have destroyed the regime from within irrespective of the suppression of the Hama revolt. Despite the fact the Syrian rebels were specifically appealing to a Sunni constituency, Assad appears to have turned to Iran to delegitimize the opposition. Given Iran's revolutionary credentials and its Islamic appeal, Iranian support for Assad may have helped to contain the internal repercussions of the showdown with Ikhwan. Assad's success may have had more to do with the maintenance of loyalty within the army than with any proclamation from Tehran; nonetheless, and despite Ikhwan appeals to the contrary, Iran publicly decided to give precedence to its state-to-state relationship with Syria over its putative ideological affinity with a sibling Islamic, albeit Sunni, revolutionary movement.

After Hama, both states moved quickly towards an official alliance. A far-reaching trade and economic protocol between the two countries was signed by Syrian Vice-President Khaddam in Tehran in March 1982 (although it had most probably been negotiated in the months prior to Hama). The agreement included the annual export of 9 million tonnes of Iranian oil to Syria, with some 20,000 barrels/day gratis and other discounts, and a reciprocal export of Syrian phosphate to Iran. The reason behind Iran's economic largesse in spite of its own pressing war needs became evident a month later when Syria first closed its borders with Iraq and then shut down the vital Iraqi–Syrian oil pipeline from Kirkuk to Banias and Tripoli in North Lebanon, thus reducing Iraqi oil exports by half and adding an estimated $7 billion annual loss to Iraq's war costs. A series of successful Iranian spring offensives coinciding with the Syrian–Iranian agreements may have benefited from unannounced new Syrian arms shipments appended to the deal.

Syria's appreciation of the importance of its alliance with Iran as a balancing element in the region was most probably sharpened by the completion of the Israeli evacuation of Sinai in April 1982, clearly indicating that the Egyptian–Israeli peace treaty would be fully implemented despite the assassination of President Sadat the previous October and putting an end to whatever lingering Syrian/Arab hopes there remained of reversing the Camp David process.

Israel's invasion of Lebanon

By the middle of 1982 the Syrian–Iranian alliance appeared to have begun seriously to affect Iraq's war prospects. But in June Syria was diverted elsewhere, and with this diversion a new Iranian role in the area began to take shape. Israel's invasion of Lebanon that summer transformed the strategic landscape in the Mashriq. While the immediate object of the invasion was to uproot the PLO from the Lebanese arena, its grander objective was to humble Syria militarily and dislodge Lebanon from Syria's sphere of interest and control. Though these objectives did not necessarily form the consensual ground rules for the invasion within Israel itself (as the ever-growing internal Israeli opposition to the Begin government's Lebanese adventure was to show), Syrian insecurities were undoubtedly multiplied by Israel's initial military successes and its apparent ambitions. Syria's acute sense of vulnerability was highlighted by a number of factors. First, there was the humiliating defeat and dispersal of the PLO, an 'objective' ally of Syria and one operating under its grand strategic protection, political differences notwithstanding. Second, and possibly even more important from a Syrian point of view, there was the devastating demonstration of Israeli technological superiority over the Syrian air force, which lost 102 aircraft and 61 pilots killed in three days, and the almost effortless destruction of Syria's surface-to-air missile system, which had previously provided some sense of security from the long reach of Israeli airpower. Third was the conspicuous absence of any real Arab or international support, most critically of any effective political or military response from Syria's strategic ally, the Soviet Union. Soviet caution regarding the Israeli invasion and Syria's military predicament only reinforced Syria's perception of the limitations of the Soviet role in the area. Fourth, and equally ominous, was the emerging alliance between Israel and the successive Phalangist regimes of Bashir and Amin Gemayel respectively. This alliance threatened to place a pro-Israeli minority government on Syria's flank with full US blessing and support, thus potentially reviving long-standing Sunni suspicions about minority loyalties only months after the Hama showdown.

Iraq's links with the Abu-Nidal group and the latter's attack on the Israeli ambassador in London in early June 1982 give some credence to the belief that this attack may have been deliberately staged by Iraq to spur a Syrian–Israeli showdown in retaliation for Syria's increasingly damaging support for Iran. The Israeli invasion would almost certainly have gone ahead with any other minimally credible *casus belli*, regardless of Iraqi actions or intentions; nevertheless, after 1982 and for the next few years Syria's preoccupation with the Lebanese-Israeli-Palestinian arena was almost all-encompassing, and to that extent Iraq's possible objective of containing Syrian involvement in the war with Iran may have been achieved. But the 1982 invasion also had a profound affect on Iran's presence in Lebanon and by extension on its role in the Arab–Israeli conflict. The invasion provided the opportunity for the first direct Iranian contribution to the anti-Israeli war effort in the form of a relatively small contingent of some 800–1,000 (some estimates put the figure at 1,500) *Pasdaran* (revolutionary guards) allowed through Syria into the presumed friendly environment of the Shia area of Baalbeck in the Bikaa Valley. Previously, Iranian attempts to install an independent military presence in Lebanon had apparently been blocked by Assad himself, but the Syrian posture just after the Israeli invasion was probably less resistant to Iranian offers of help than before. Iran's offer of active support contrasted sharply with the virtual immobility of the rest of the Arab world and the Soviet Union. Arab inaction confirmed the value of the Iranian link in Syrian eyes and reinforced Syrian perceptions that the post-Camp David era necessitated a strategic realignment that could constrain Israel's ever-widening margins of manoeuvre (particularly in Lebanon), with Iran as Syria's only remotely credible partner in the arena.

From Iran's point of view, its new presence in Lebanon afforded the first direct point of contact between the revolutionary regime and a major Shiite community in the Arab world – the largest such community outside Iraq. Henceforth, Iran would become a leading player in this community and would consider it a potential base for projecting its influence into the heart of the Arab–Israeli conflict. The exact role of Lebanon in the ongoing debate between those in Tehran who sought to export the revolution across the area and those who had more limited objectives remains unclear. However, this initial Iranian presence in Lebanon appears to have been supported by the more 'radical' wing, as represented by Ayatollah Ali Akkbar Mohtashami, then the Iranian ambassador in Damascus, who was also responsible for the Lebanese arena.

Two processes quickly converged. First, Lebanese Shiite politics were subject to new fissures as a result of the emergence of local pro-Iranian elements. The hitherto almost total domination of the scene by Amal gave way as its more radical constituency naturally gravitated towards the Iranian model and its first organizational manifestations, such as Hussein Mussawi's Islamic Amal, founded as a breakaway group of Amal in June 1982. Suffering from the loss of the energetic and charismatic Musa al-Sadr, who had 'disappeared' in somewhat mysterious circumstances after a visit to Libya in 1978, and who had sought to minimize the influence of the Shia clergy as a means of containing their perceived sectarian and competitive influence within the organization, Amal appeared incapable of containing the new Shiite forces unleashed by the Israeli invasion. By 1982 Amal was essentially in non-religious hands, as represented by Sadr's lacklustre successor Nabih Berri, and was structurally and ideologically ill-prepared to concede a role to the radicalized Shiite clergy. The radical religious elements thus found increasing ideological common ground with Iran and its local representatives, and looked beyond Amal for an organizational channel for their political discourse and activity. Second, a new, largely Shiite resistance movement drawn from such elements began to take shape in southern Lebanon. This resistance, which was eventually to mount the most effective guerrilla campaign ever waged against Israel (and in part against the Western military presence in Lebanon), represented the first operational testing ground for the alliance between Syria and Iran.

Israel's occupation of substantial tracts of southern Lebanon (up to and including West Beirut during the first phase of operations) had a profound impact on Israeli relations with the Lebanese Shia, and consequently on the roles of both Syria and Iran in Lebanon. At first, Shia disillusionment with the PLO, combined with the relative absence of a distinctly 'Shiite' historical animosity towards Israel, seemed to open a brief window of opportunity for an Israeli–Shia detente. Indeed, Amal's position regarding the Israeli military presence in Lebanon remained ambivalent for some time, partly out of conviction that this presence was impermanent, and partly because Amal's leadership was cautiously weighing up its prospects in the new Maronite-dominated Lebanese order supported by the United States and Israel. The damage wrought on Shia areas by the invasion during the previous years of conflict, the political divergence between the PLO and Amal over issues relating to the civil war since 1975–6 and the disdain felt for the PLO's military performance during the Israeli invasion had all contributed to a certain sense of Shiite relief at the eviction of the PLO from Lebanon – a sense not uncommon among other presumed allies of the Palestinians in the immediate aftermath of the invasion. Underlying this sense was a feeling that the PLO, as the dominant Sunni force on the Muslim/left side, had helped to tilt the Lebanese politico-sectarian balance against Amal and the Shia and in favour of the Sunnis. Added to this was the widening rift between the PLO and Syria after June 1982, which minimized Amal's incentives to rekindle any latent links with or sympathies for the PLO.

To the more radical Shiite elements, however, the Israeli occupation of what were mostly Shia areas represented a direct challenge, regardless of the state of relations with the Palestinians. Fired by Iran's ideological stance, by the very fact of occupation and by a readiness for self-sacrifice and martyrdom, the radical Shia helped to form the basis for a new dimension to the Syrian–Iranian alliance. In lieu of the Palestinian–Israeli confrontation that had dominated the course of events in Lebanon for almost a decade and a half, a Shiite-led war of liberation was about to commence. The 'Sunni' cause of Palestine thus began to merge with the Shia's own independent cause: that of resistance to Israeli occupation.

After the invasion: a broadening of interests

At this time the coincidence of interests and outlook between Syria and Iran began to broaden. In its campaign to drive the Israelis out of Lebanon, Syria's immediate motives were strategic: the Israeli military presence in the southern half of Lebanon and specifically in the Bikaa Valley put the Syrian heartland under a dual threat. For the first time Damascus itself was in potential double jeopardy from both the Golan and the forward Israeli positions in Lebanon. In addition, there was the geopolitical threat emanating from a pro-Western and pro-Israeli regime in Lebanon. Syrian concern about the possibility of regional isolation and the dangers of separate bilateral Arab–Israeli deals was then, as now, a primary determinant of its foreign policy. A Lebanon in the Israeli–US orbit would further tilt the already unfavourable regional balance by complementing the Iraqi and Israeli threats with a possible encirclement from the west. Lebanon's defection would add its weight to the loss of Egypt, and given the uncertain position of Jordan, the pressure on Syria to accept yet another Arab humiliation along the lines of Camp David would become severe. In this respect the May 1983 Lebanese–Israeli accord brokered by the United States was almost tailor-made to feed Syrian suspicions. Equally, a hostile Lebanon could become the base for internal subversion, leading to sectarian strife and a breakdown of internal stability within Syria itself. Syria's fears of possible Israeli or Western support for the fragmentation of the area into subservient or mutually competing sectarian entities had been highlighted by the

17

Israeli–Maronite alliance, and by Israel's post-1982 flirtation with the Lebanese Druze, all with apparent US collusion or consent.

Under these circumstances Syria's desire to strengthen its ties with Iran is unsurprising. For the momentous task of reshaping the strategic landscape to its advantage, Syria could rely on Iran to provide material help in the form of economic aid, manpower in the form of a ready-made local constituency, motivation in the form of a radical anti-Israeli and anti-Western outlook, and a new source of pressure and potential threat to divert almost all Syria's regional and international adversaries, while remaining at sufficient physical and historical distance to avoid becoming too powerful or too independent on Syria's home turf.

For its part, Iran's interests reflected a number of separate but interrelated factors. Despite its new activism in Lebanon, Iran's supreme concern still centred on the pursuit of the war against Iraq. By mid-1982 Iraq had withdrawn all its forces from Iranian soil and the Iranians had begun to threaten Iraq proper with a series of offensives aimed at Basra. No longer a clear victim of aggression but apparently bent on a punitive prolongation of the war against Iraq, Iran's offensives severely strained whatever good relations remained with its initial Arab friends, such as Algeria and the People's Democratic Republic of Yemen (PDRY). Iran's need for a reliable ally was therefore that much more acute given its desire to keep a significant foothold in the Arab camp and its need to maintain pressure on Iraq. Notwithstanding Syria's official disapproval of any Iranian *territorial* war aims in Iraq, from the Iranian point of view there was no real substitute for preserving the alliance with Syria. After the 1982 Israeli invasion, Iran's interests tended to converge with Syria's in the Lebanese arena. Iran was primarily motivated by its deep doctrinal hostility to Israel and the bitter legacy of the latter's ties to the Shah; but the prospect of gaining a point of entry into the Arab–Israeli conflict also opened the door for a more substantial regional role. Through its presence in the Lebanon, Iran could hope to break out of the narrow geopolitical confines of the war with Iraq and reach a wider constituency within the Arab world. While Iran's Shiite concerns were naturally pivotal to its Lebanese policy, its active support for the struggle against Israel was also central to the Iranian revolution's pan-Islamic appeal. Although it is difficult to determine the exact nature of Iranian expectations regarding the prospects for 'exporting' the revolution, the Lebanese arena was crucial both in strictly Shiite terms and as a base for activism elsewhere in the area. The final element was that of Iranian hostility to the extension of US and Western power into Lebanon. Iran's struggle with the United States was an integral part of the symbolism and practice of the revolution – as witnessed in the taking of US embassy hostages in Tehran – and the continuing conflict in Lebanon afforded the possibility of pursuing this struggle, later to be seriously aggravated by the US 'tilt' towards Iraq.

None of these Iranian goals necessarily contradicted Syrian objectives as a matter of principle. In practice, however, relations between the two were not always fully harmonious.

The Syrian–Iranian counteroffensive

Prompted partly by their own local motivations but equally by a complex of anti-Israeli motives and strategic concerns, Syria and Iran sought the appropriate means to pursue their aims. Henceforth, both Syria and Iran would find common utility in cultivating their relations with the various Lebanese parties as proxy forces against common enemies – and occasionally against each other. The range of potential targets for such proxies was wide; but first and foremost were the Israeli occupation forces. Initially, a loose cooperative structure known as the the the Lebanese National Resistance (LNR) acted as a broad front for both Iranian- and Syrian-backed elements including the then nascent Hizbullah and certain sections within Amal, as well as components of the Lebanese National Movement and the remnants of the Palestinian military presence, both pro- and anti-Arafat. The exact degree of military cooperation within the LNR remains uncertain, as does the nature of command and logistical support provided by either Syria or Iran, but it was more a politically convenient fiction than a truly cohesive military organization.

Iran's access to the field of operations could only have been made possible through Syrian acquiescence. Syria, however, operating in its own backyard and totally committed to undoing the negative results of the Israeli invasion as a matter of vital national interest, was from the outset unwilling to cede anti-Israeli operations to the Iranian-backed elements alone. One of Syria's concerns was not to tip the balance too sharply against Amal within the Shiite community while gaining the greatest possible leverage from the radical wing of the movement in so far as it spearheaded the increasingly effective military campaign against Israel's occupation. Iran was of great use as a means of encouraging and inspiring such activity, but it was not in the Syrian scheme of things to allow it a totally autonomous foothold in Lebanon that could undermine Syria's own position. To some extent, both Syria and Iran had begun to compete for the same natural constituencies. Alongside the Lebanese Shiite community, these included other secular radical elements such the anti-Arafat Palestinian factions then emerging from the Syrian-backed split within Fateh in early 1983. The potential for friction between Syria and Iran thus began to increase at the very point at which they began active collaboration in Lebanon.

The Israelis were not the only targets of proxy action. Multiple attacks were carried out on Western targets in Lebanon by suspected Syrian–Iranian proxies, commencing with the first bombing of the US embassy in Beirut in April 1983 and continuing through the destruction of the French and US Marine barracks in October of that year and the wave of hostage-taking that began in 1984. To the Israelis and the other Western powers these operations (as 'suicide' attacks) seemed to indicate the arrival of a particularly deadly and implacable form of hostile action, compared with which the old-established forms of Palestinian 'terrorism' seemed almost tame.

By the time these and other operations had effectively beaten the Israelis back into the Security Zone unilaterally declared by Israel in southern Lebanon in the spring of 1985, the Syrian–Iranian counter-offensive in Lebanon had achieved remarkable success in neutralizing the results of the 1982 invasion. First, it blocked the fruition of intensive US diplomacy aimed at converting Israel's initial military gains into permanent political and diplomatic advantage. Only months after its signing, the May 1983 Israeli–Lebanese accord – the second Arab–Israeli peace treaty after Camp David – had petered into insignificance and irrelevancy. Second, and following this diplomatic defeat, the United States led the multinational evacuation of Lebanon in February 1984 in response to the blowing up of the Marine barracks in Beirut – a blow that still resonates today in its effect on US willingness to commit its forces overseas. Third, and in tandem with the US pull-out, Amal swept back into West Beirut, indirectly re-establishing Syria's dominion in the Lebanese capital. Last but not least, and with the defeat of Arafat's ill-fated Tripoli expedition in late 1983, Syria had successfully ended the prospect of an effective independent Palestinian presence in Lebanon.

Amal in particular stands out as a malleable instrument of Syrian policy – though not without its own imperatives – in confronting the Lebanese government and its allies of the (Christian) 'Lebanese Forces', in participating in the anti-Israeli resistance and in competing with the pro-Iranian radicals within its own community. But the variety of proxy roles in this period is instructive. Syrian-backed Palestinian proxies (Jibril's PFLP-GC) fought against the PLO; Druze militia allied to Syria joined hands with Fateh elements in evicting the Lebanese Forces from the Shouf area; Syrian–Iranian proxies appear to have borne the brunt of covert operations against Israeli and Western targets; and Israel itself went about strengthening its own Maronite–Shiite proxy force in the shape of the SLA (South Lebanon Army) to bear the burden of guarding and protecting the Security Zone. None of this precluded the direct and non-proxy confrontations involving almost every force on Lebanese soil up to and including the bombing of Syrian positions in the Bikaa Valley by US and French warplanes in December 1983.

Syrian–Iranian tensions in Lebanon

The achievements of 1982–4 also had their costs. The Iranian agenda in Lebanon had always been subject to the push and pull of different tendencies in Tehran itself, which in turn could affect the state of Syrian–Iranian relations. While Syria sought to maintain its traditional policy of balancing the different Lebanese parties against each other and to keep Lebanon within the generally secular Syrian orbit, the public emergence of Hizbullah in September 1984 marked a new watershed. From a Syrian point of view this development was problematic. On the one hand the radical pro-Iranian elements formed the most effective arm of proxy activity against Israel and the United States; on the other, the call for an Islamic republic in Lebanon and the subjugation of Hizbullah's will to the spiritual and political dictates of Tehran – though the latter were not always clear or consistent – were potentially at direct odds with established Syrian interests.

The first severe test of the alliance came over Syrian policy towards the Palestinians. Worried about pro-Arafat Fateh infiltration of the Beirut camps and the possibility of an Arafat–Lebanese Forces link-up, Syria gave Amal free reign to surround and subjugate the camps. A protracted and ugly conflict developed through various phases from May/June 1985 until February 1987. Amal's rationale for leading this campaign was based not only on its calculus of self-interest *vis-à-vis* the Syrians, but on a bitter rejection of any return to the pre-1982 status quo regarding an autonomous Palestinian presence in Lebanon. Hizbullah, by way of contrast, stood against this policy of forcible reduction of the Palestinians on both ideological and political grounds. Despite the steady deterioration of PLO–Iranian relations since 1980 and the PLO's stance in support of Iraq in the Iran–Iraq war, Hizbullah's commitment to the Palestinian cause ran deep (the public announcement of Hizbullah's birth had been deliberately timed to mark the second anniversary of the massacre of Palestinians at Sabra and Shatilla). For Hizbullah, Amal's actions also tarnished the Shiites' good name, thus directly affecting the Iranian revolution's profile in the area and undermining the recent achievements of the struggle in Lebanon.

The dispute over the 'war of the camps' was also related to a broader dispute over the next phase of the guerrilla campaign. As the Israeli military presence retreated into the Security Zone, Amal policy in South Lebanon (largely inspired by local Amal leaders such as Daoud Daoud) turned increasingly towards a pragmatic *modus vivendi* with Israel: in return for a tacit acceptance of the new status quo, Amal's southern fiefdom was not to be used as a springboard for attacks on either the Security Zone or Israel itself. Hizbullah, however, was bent on pressing forward with its campaign to liberate Lebanese soil from Israeli occupation. The 'Islamic Resistance' (*al-Muqawammah al-Islamiyayah*) formed by Hizbullah in 1985 was a clear indication of its determination to pursue the struggle under the unequivocal banner of Islam and Iran. Henceforth the vast majority of operations against the Israelis and the SLA in the Security Zone would be attributed to Hizbullah.

The 'war of the camps' in Beirut led to an intensive Iranian diplomatic effort to end the bloodshed. This involved repeated high-level Iranian visits and consultations with the Syrians as well as with the local parties themselves. At times Hizbullah actively intervened on the Palestinian side and otherwise provided the hard-pressed Palestinians with food and other supplies. But Syria's determination to uproot the final vestiges of Arafat's power – particularly in Beirut – was unshakeable. In addition, Syria may have sought to underline the limits of Iranian and pro-Iranian power to Tehran and Hizbullah alike. An Iranian–Hizbullah success in preventing Syria from implementing its policy in Lebanon would have sent a dangerous message regarding the relative power of each actor in the Lebanese arena. The Syrian incentive to draw firm and mutually understood limits to this power in the aftermath of the joint campaign of 1983–4 was also strong. Yet Syria's toleration of Hizbullah's anti-Israeli activity in South Lebanon showed no marked change in this period and remains undiminished to this day. Within certain limitations, the Syrian tendency to balance one role against another has been a permanent characteristic of its Lebanon policy.

Between 1986 and 1989 Syrian–Iranian relations faced a number of crises, exacerbated by a series of underlying conflicts. First, both sides were weary of the role played by the other's allies and proxies in

Lebanon. The growth of Hizbullah in Lebanon as a potent military force was matched by its emergence as an effective and energetic patron of an extensive network of social and welfare services unavailable from any other source. Between 1982 and 1986, when the Syrian–Iranian counter-offensive in Lebanon was at its height, an estimated $90 million of Iranian grants were disbursed by Hizbullah's Martyr's Foundation (*Muassasat as-Shaheed*) to the families of those killed or wounded during the campaign. In the period 1985–7 alone, Hizbullah announced the establishment of 2 major hospitals, 16 infirmaries, 2 dental clinics, 3 pharmacies and 6 civil defence centres in the predominantly Shiite areas of the Bikaa, Beirut's southern suburbs and various parts of South Lebanon. By 1989, around 70,000 patients were being received and treated annually in one hospital for women and children. Hizbullah's challenge to Syrian dominance among the Shia in Lebanon thus went beyond operational differences over the Palestinians and the war in the south, and had begun to strike at the very foundation of Syrian influence and prestige.

Second, Syrian–Iranian differences spilled over into other aspects of the Lebanese arena. One of the knock-on effects of Shia radicalization after 1982 had been the growth of a Sunni fundamentalist movement, most active in the north Lebanon town of Tripoli. The Tawhid party under Sheikh Said Shaban preached the same non-sectarian Islamic message as its Shia counterparts and formed an active alliance with Hizbullah with support and encouragement from the PLO. For Syria, the combination of Shaban, Arafat and Hizbullah was particularly ominous inasmuch as it brought together Shia and Sunni radicals with powerful external patrons. The loss of Tripoli would have been particularly dangerous given the city's proximity to Syria and its traditionally strong influence on northern Lebanese politics as well as its concerns for the local Alawite minority. Syrian–Tawhid clashes in 1985 continued into 1986 alongside rising Iranian disapproval of Syria's attempt to put down Shaban by force, adding to the existing tensions over the war of the camps and the competition between Amal and Hizbullah.

Third, the economic agreements between the two countries started to run into serious difficulties. As a result of Iraqi aerial attacks on Iran's oil export terminals at Kharg, Iranian oil production had hit an all-time low by spring 1986, while Syria's own economic difficulties had led to the accumulation of an estimated $970 million debt to Iran since 1982. Starting in 1985, Iran began to delay oil shipments to exert pressure on Syria to repay its mounting debt, and in early 1986 it stopped Syrian oil shipments altogether for the first time.

Assad's handling of these tensions with Tehran is instructive. On the one hand, Syria responded favourably to a Saudi initiative regarding a rapprochement with Jordan – by then one of Iraq's closest allies and active supporters. The success of this Saudi initiative in turn raised the prospect of a Jordanian-brokered meeting between Assad and Saddam. Iranian concern about the mere possibility of such a Syrian move towards Iraq facilitated a rapid and satisfactory renegotiation of the economic package and the reassertion of the alliance in late summer 1986. On the other hand, Syria was not ready to stand idle as Hizbullah's power and influence in Lebanon expanded. In February 1987 Syrian troops clashed directly with Hizbullah in Beirut's southern suburbs. A few weeks later, in April 1987, substantial evidence emerged of a Saudi-sponsored meeting between Assad and Saddam. Although this summit was never officially confirmed and had no lasting effect, the combination of a possible Syrian opening to Iraq and a firm policy towards Hizbullah and Tawhid seems to have confronted the Iranians with the reality of their limited leverage with Syria. When large-scale fighting broke out between Amal and Hizbullah in May 1988, Iran attempted to mediate an end to the violence in full consultation with the Syrians, paving the way for the first Syrian deployment of troops in Beirut's southern suburbs (Hizbullah's strongholds) since 1982.

One vital area of joint Iranian–Syrian interest, and a source of potential conflict, had to do with the Western hostages taken in Lebanon. Although the Iranian government maintained its distance from the operational elements involved, its influence with the hostage-takers was deemed sufficient to prompt the US–Israeli opening to Iran which culminated in the Iran–Contra scandal. Syria's alleged links to the 1986 attempt to blow up an Israeli airliner on a flight from London (the Hindawi affair) and its official classification on the US 'terrorist' list rankled for both psychological and practical reasons. Both sides thus sought to deny any collusion with terrorism and yet to derive maximum advantage from US and Western sensitivities regarding the hostages. A release of hostages could facilitate relations with the Western side and elicit some *quid pro quo*, as with the hostages-for-arms swap with Iran, and the mere presence of hostages in areas nominally within the sphere of Syrian and/or Iranian influence guaranteed a certain amount of outside interest and engagement with either or both countries concerned. In guarding its turf as *the* major channel for a hostage release, Syria actively sought to curtail Iran's ability to strike a separate deal in this regard. The first leak of the Iran–Contra deal by the pro-Syrian media in Lebanon in 1986 was thus meant not only to abort any renewal of Iranian relations with Israel and the United States, but equally to reassert Syria's indispensability in resolving the hostage crisis. Nonetheless, Syria's embarrassment over its inability to prevent hostages being taken or to ensure their rapid subsequent release was occasionally acute. The line between ensuring outside acknowledgment of Syrian and Iranian influence in Lebanon and being held directly responsible for events occurring there was not always an easy one to tread; and the hostages appeared to demonstrate the limits of both Syrian and Iranian leverage with their ostensible allies in Lebanon.

The longevity of the hostage crisis reflected in part the complexity of personal, sectarian, ideological and party relations within the local factions and between them and their external sponsors. This in turn also reflected the lack of any clear chain of command or definitive source of authority over the pro-Iranian elements in Lebanon. However, the Iranians appear to have held the decisive key to ending the crisis, despite the importance of Syria's role in Lebanon. Eventually, when Iranian national interests dictated that all hostages be released in 1990–1, neither the competing centres of power in Tehran nor the autonomous aspirations of the Lebanese radical elements were sufficient to prevent the releases being pushed through.

The end of the Iran–Iraq war

Iran's compensation for its (eventual) readiness to concede Syrian dominance in Lebanon lay elsewhere. Despite the importance of the Lebanese arena, Iran's vital strategic interest was to maintain Syrian support in the war against Iraq. Since 1984 and the 'tanker war', an increasingly active US military role in the Gulf posed new dangers to Iran, while the war with Iraq offered no clear evidence of a possible Iranian military breakthrough. During 1985–6 the covert attempt by the United States to re-establish ties with Iran – prompted and encouraged by Israel in the hope of rekindling pre-Shah ties with certain elements in the Iranian establishment – had done little to diminish the suspicion between Iran and the United States. Although Iran was probably unaware that the United States had been providing Iraq with access to high-grade photo and signals intelligence regarding Iranian troop dispositions since 1983, the dominant attitude remained one of unmitigated hostility towards both the United States itself and its allies in the area. Iranian intractability regarding Iraq put pressure on Syria's Arab relations. Syria found itself in a progressively more difficult position defending Iran in Arab fora, culminating in the adoption of the Amman Arab Summit's condemnation of Iran in November 1987 (Syria attempted to limit the damage to its relations with Tehran by refraining from publishing the Summit's resolutions in its news media).

Syria's continued alliance with Iran in spite of these public difficulties reflected a number of considerations. The first was the danger of slackening the pressure on Saddam. Syrian support for Iran deepened the rift with Iraq and increased the likelihood of Iraqi retaliation against Syria should the opportunity arise; a break-up of the alliance with Iran would have done little to placate Saddam at this late stage and Syria may have judged that it was better to keep Iran as a counterweight to Iraq than rely on Iraqi gratitude for a belated change in the relationship with Tehran. Second, and despite appearances, Syria's link with Iran gave it both regional and international leverage. The Gulf states in particular appeared ready to maintain their economic aid to Syria and tacitly acknowledged the utility of the Syrian channel to Iran. At the same time, the mere threat of a possible rapprochement with Saddam gave Syria considerable leverage with Iran itself. Without having to undertake anything more than a few symbolic steps in this direction (as the Assad–Saddam meeting of April 1987 showed), Syria could put pressure on Iran and satisfy its Arab constituency at one and the same time. Third, the emergence of two major Arab blocs in the mid-1980s, the Arab Cooperation Council (comprising Egypt, Iraq, Jordan and North Yemen) and the six Gulf Cooperation Council (GCC) states (Saudi Arabia, Kuwait, Bahrain, Qatar, the United Arab Emirates and Oman), aggravated the Syrian sense of regional isolation. In this context, Iran continued to provide Syria with a powerful partner and alternative pole.

Between August 1988 and August 1990 a number of developments affected the Syrian–Iranian relationship. The end of the Iran–Iraq war appeared to strengthen Iraq's hand considerably *vis-à-vis* both Syria and Iran. Iraq had not only succeeded in forcing a humiliating end to the war by demonstrating its almost complete military superiority over Iran, but was very well positioned to make best use of its broad international and Arab support to act as the major Arab power astride the Gulf and the Mashriq. Iran's incentives to cling to the alliance with Syria were thus reinforced by a combination of its own weakness, Iraqi power, US military projection into the Gulf (such as the flagging of Kuwaiti ships and escorting tankers through Gulf waters) and regional and international isolation. Syria was likewise motivated by its traditional interest in containing Iraq and maintaining its unique role in Lebanon. But other factors were at work too, first and foremost the changes in East–West relations and the diminution of US–Soviet rivalry in the area. Syria's long-standing political and strategic relationship with the Soviet Union had begun to erode with the advent of President Gorbachev in the mid-1980s and the increasing Soviet reluctance to subsidize Syria's military efforts or bail out its ailing economy. The Soviet Union's own changing agenda put pressure on the Syrians to reconsider their grand strategy towards Israel, including the doctrine of strategic parity developed by the Syrians in the wake of the Camp David accords (see Chapter 3). Based on the assumption of Syrian military strength and an upper ceiling of Israeli freedom of action delimited by an implicit Soviet deterrent, the 1982 experience in Lebanon had called into question the credibility of the putative Soviet security umbrella. By April 1987 Gorbachev was telling Assad in Moscow that 'strategic parity' in the sense of military equivalence with Israel was a chimera and that the continued severance of Soviet–Israeli diplomatic ties was an 'abnormal' state of affairs. While the Soviet Union had done much since 1982 to help bolster Syrian defensive capabilities, the notion that Syria could maintain a credible offensive posture was henceforth significantly downgraded. The Syrian–Soviet relationship, a mainstay of Syrian foreign and defence policy since the mid-1950s, was undergoing a substantial transformation. The comparison with the blossoming US–Israeli strategic alliance emerging out of the Reagan years was stark. All the more reason, then, for Syria to seek to maintain its alliance with Iran – especially as, after the end of the war with Iran, Iraq's attempt at retribution against Syria was not long coming, in the shape of support for the 'war of liberation' against Syria's presence in Lebanon led by the head of the Lebanese army, General Michel Aoun. Eventually, however, Aoun's resistance crumbled and he fled Lebanon under the combined weight of Syrian military pressure, deep divisions within the Maronite camp and US ambivalence towards Aounist adventurism. A Saudi-brokered and US–backed deal in Taif at the end of 1989 finally re-established the delicate sectarian rules of the game in Lebanon in a manner consistent with Syria's perceived interests, and paved the way for an end to Lebanese internal strife.

The death of Ayatollah Khomeini in the summer of 1989 had its effect on the central direction of Iranian foreign policy and on Iranian relations with the various components of the Shia movement in Lebanon. The election of President Rafsanjani led to a discernible interest in broadening the base of Iran's contacts in Lebanon, manifesting itself in a closer relationship between Iran and Amal. Concurrently, Hizbullah itself was starting to reassess its role within the Lebanese polity. Hizbullah's conception of its mission as a *Lebanese* organization and not merely as an external appendage of Iran was strengthened by the independent-mindedness of Sheikh Fadlallah and the post-Khomeini vacuum in Shiite political and jurisprudential authority. Against this background, and although clearly weary of an Iraqi-backed Maronite regime in Lebanon, Iran and Hizbullah were not entirely content with the Taif accords. The Aoun crisis had highlighted common Syrian–Iranian interests in Lebanon, but also the areas of potential tension between them. Both Iran and Hizbullah appear to have been cut out of the process of consultations leading to the Taif accords, sponsored largely through a tripartite committee of Algeria, Morocco and Saudi Arabia, discreetly supported by the United States. For Iran, this seemed to confirm Syria's readiness to exclude it from what could be considered an 'Arab' affair, thus relegating Iranian interests in Lebanon to a relatively secondary place. Equally, the accords themselves did not give the Lebanese Shia what Iran and Hizbullah considered their due, especially in the light of their struggles and sacrifices after the 1982 invasion. Nonetheless, and despite some contradictory initial comments reflecting the internal debate in Tehran, Iran's interest in avoiding a break with Syria led Tehran to reassure Syria of its support for the accords.

These tensions in Syrian–Iranian relations should also be put in the context of wider developments on the Arab scene. Continued Iranian opposition to Syria in Lebanon could only have strengthened Iraq's hand at both parties' expense. It was thus clearly in neither side's interest to pursue this path. Iran's defeat in the war against Iraq had upset the inter-Arab regional balance by leaving Syria unprotected against a confident and apparently increasingly internationally well-placed Saddam. In addition, the new pragmatism of President Rafsanjani may have caused the Syrians some concern. First, it might portend a possible rapprochement with the West or the Gulf. This would undermine Syria's interest in acting as a potential mediator on Iran's behalf, as well as possibly opening the door for a breakaway Iranian policy that could derogate from Syria's role as the pragmatic radical actor in the area. Second, such Iranian pragmatism could make inroads into Syria's Shiite base in Lebanon outside Hizbullah. Third, its ultimate direction regarding Iraq was uncertain. Although it was safe to assume that the legacy of the war with Iraq would not dissipate overnight, a truly pragmatic Iran (or one too self-absorbed in internal reconstruction) could allow for a broader margin of Iraqi freedom of action in domains that were not vital from an Iranian point of view but that were of supreme interest to Syria. Such concerns may be seen behind Syria's opening to Egypt and the resumption of diplomatic relations between the two countries in late 1989. Despite Syrian bitterness at Egypt's betrayal at Camp David, the need to counterbalance Iraq was a vital Syrian interest with the apparent waning of Iranian power and activism. Feeding off local, especially Gulf, fears of Iraqi ambitions and good Egyptian–Gulf relations, Syria was also better placed to pose itself as a potential counterbalance to Iraq by improving its relations with Egypt.

The second Gulf war

Iraq's invasion of Kuwait in August 1990 provided what could have been the most serious test yet of the Syrian–Iranian relationship. Yet while Syria's support of military intervention against Iraq within the context of a *US-led* coalition was a remarkably deft political and diplomatic achievement on the part of Assad, it was perhaps even more remarkable that Iran should have accepted the deployment of Syrian troops alongside their American counterparts in Operation Desert Storm with relative equanimity and no visible negative effect on the relationship between the two countries.

The Kuwait crisis offered a vital opportunity to defeat Saddam and finally do away with his persistent threat to Syria and Iran alike. In this respect, Syria's alignment with the United States (and the 'conservative' Arab regimes) provided Iran with the vicarious means to achieve its long-standing ideological and strategic goal. Iran's apparent readiness to accept Syria's new relationship with the United States may be set against persistent Iranian fears that the next US-led military action in the area would be directed against Iran itself. Syria could thus act as a restraining influence on the United States and as a possible obstacle to its freedom of action against Iran. Through Syria, Iran could also maintain an indirect foothold in the anti-Saddam coalition without having to compromise itself directly. Conversely, Iran's tacit acquiescence in the anti-Saddam coalition gave it new leverage with all concerned. Iran not only replenished its air force with a considerable quantity of modern aircraft flown there direct from Iraq, but also extracted an Iraqi reaffirmation of the 1975 Shatt al-Arab agreement, unilaterally abrogated by Saddam in 1980. Iran's position with the rest of the Gulf and the West in 1990–1 also benefited from a reinforcement of the view that it was slowly evolving away from its previously radical stance and that it could not be ignored as a major player in the Gulf.

From the Syrian point of view, the position of Iran during the Kuwait crisis appeared to vindicate Syria's persistence in maintaining close relations with Tehran over the years. However, it was necessary to ensure that there would be no chance of a Syrian–Iranian misunderstanding as a result of Assad's policy towards the crisis. It was no coincidence, therefore, that Assad's only post-revolutionary visit to Tehran took place on 20–25 September 1990. Indeed, there is some evidence to suggest that Syria may have sought to test out Iranian responses to military action against Iraq and to engage Iran more directly in support of the coalition by deploying troops in Saudi Arabia. From an Arab–US perspective, one possible worst-case scenario was an Iraqi–Iranian political or military coalition that would take an active stand against the use of force to evict Iraq from Kuwait. In the event, Assad's visit helped to bolster confidence within the coalition that the immediate regional repercussions of a military move against Saddam would be limited. Saddam's attempt to appeal to Islam and the radical Islamic constituency in the area was also at least partly undermined by the joint stance of Syria and Iran. Given the influence of both parties with a wide range of Islamic and secular radical groups, Iraq's failure to mobilize any serious popular or 'terrorist' effort on its behalf may be largely attributed to a conscious Syrian–Iranian policy of restraint in this domain.

The second Gulf war provided solid evidence of the durability of the Syrian–Iranian relationship. It also showed the vital importance of the Iraqi factor in the strategic calculations of both sides. The Damascus Declaration which brought together the six GCC countries with Egypt and Syria in 1991 (6+2) initially suggested that an Arab collective security approach to the Gulf would emerge from the war, with both Syria and Egypt playing a major military role in the area for the first time. This project was to flounder almost immediately, primarily as a result of continued Gulf reluctance to cede the role of protector to any external party besides the United States. Unlike Egypt, Syria itself did not set great store by the possibility of an active military role in Gulf security, seeking instead a broader *political* role and a share of Gulf economic support. In the event, Syria's role in the Gulf was undoubtedly enhanced as a result of Desert Storm and the consolidation of regional perceptions of its balancing role against Iraq. Consequently, its value as an ally to Iran was commensurately enhanced. Syria's role as a potential bridge between Iran and the Arab Gulf states re-emerged quite quickly inasmuch as it served to re-establish Saudi–Iranian diplomatic relations in 1991 and has since continued to mitigate underlying Iranian–Gulf tensions, such as those over Abu Musa and the Tunbs. Unlike Lebanon, where Syrian–Iranian cooperation was circumscribed by open or tacit competition and the almost daily tactical frictions between the two powers and their proxies, the Gulf arena ranged over a more 'strategic' domain that was relatively free from such aggravations. At the same time, Iranian acquiescence in a Syrian role in the Gulf can be seen to echo Syria's acquiescence in an Iranian role in Lebanon, the net result being a recognition by each side that its freedom to act within the other's sphere of vital interest must remain within limits and subject to the other's final discretion. From this perspective, the second Gulf war reaffirmed the same overall utility of the Iranian–Syrian relationship regarding Iraq that had cemented their alliance during the Iran–Iraq war.

The failure of the Damascus Declaration to evolve a clear notion of Arab collective security in the Gulf may have been propitious from the point of view of the Syrian–Iranian relationship. For the Iranians, any formula granting non-Gulf powers a role in Gulf security remains both dangerous and unnecessary. Iran has consistently argued for a locally based Gulf collective security approach as a means of self-reliance as well as a bulwark against the destabilizing effect of a foreign military presence, in particular that of the United States. As originally conceived, the Damascus Declaration would not only have legitimized non-Gulf powers as bona fide players in the area but would have actively excluded Iran from what it perceived to be its rightful role in this respect. Thus a fully-fledged Syrian military role in the Gulf would not have been welcomed by Tehran, and may have been one reason why it was shelved by the Syrians themselves. The acceptable and indeed most practicable alternative for Syria has been to consolidate and pursue its political role in the Gulf, a role that remains within the boundaries of Iranian tolerance, yet allows Syria a wide margin of manoeuvre to exercise its influence and pursue its independent national political and economic interests.

Regardless of Syria's own proclivities, the eventual erosion of the Damascus Declaration formula had more to do with Gulf (particularly Saudi) sensitivities towards reducing the West's commitments in the area than with any particular aspect of Syrian Gulf policy. But Iran's own readiness to deal with Iraq is also testimony to the margins of manoeuvre retained by both parties to the alliance. Indeed, despite indications of Iraqi weakness, particularly at the time of the Kurdish uprising in northern Iraq, and the strong moral and ideological pressures created in the wake of the Shiite uprising in the south, including the bombardment of the holiest Shiite shrines in Karbala, Iran's official policy towards Iraq has been consistently level-headed since the end of the first Gulf war. In substantially weakening Saddam, the invasion of Kuwait has allowed for a more confident Iranian approach to Iraq and has allowed it to extract a certain price for any opening made towards the current regime in Baghdad at little cost to itself. At the same time, however, the Gulf war has not helped much to reduce Iranian–Arab tensions in the region, as demonstrated by the ongoing and possibly escalating conflict over Abu Musa and the Tunbs. In so far as Iran recognizes that Lebanon and the Arab–Israeli arena are of vital interest to Syria, it will be sensitive to the Syrian point of view in these domains. In return, Syria acknowledges that the Gulf arena as a whole is of vital Iranian concern. Within these basic parameters the relationship will face no fundamental threats, although this need not assume total congruence or understanding on all matters of a lesser order.

One of the most important and long-lasting shifts in the regional political environment after Desert Storm was the emerging detente between Syria and the United States. Less than six years after the US–Syrian military confrontation of 1984 in the Bikaa, the Kuwait crisis witnessed the birth of a detente that would eventually lead Syria to accept US sponsorship of the Middle East peace process; a Syrian decision that was the *sine qua non* for Arab participation in the Madrid peace conference of November 1991. This decision evolved slowly as a result of the waning role and influence of the Soviet Union, US–Syrian understanding in Lebanon regarding the Aoun rebellion and the Taif accords, Syria's estimation of the mood among other Arab actors (particularly Jordan and the PLO) and a Syrian conviction that the moment was opportune to test US intentions and policies in the area. The move towards a closer US–Syrian understanding was also a result of Syria's reading of the personal commitment to the relationship on the part of President George Bush and Secretary of State James Baker; but most of all it represented a *strategic* choice for a negotiated settlement with Israel that has become a central and irreversible element in current Syrian policy. So far at least, and despite Iran's continued opposition to a negotiated settlement, Syria's choice has not significantly impaired its relationship with Iran, giving extra credence to the belief that this is sustained by a broader and more comprehensive set of common interests.

Chapter 3

Iran, Syria and the Arab–Israeli peace process

The Iranian view of the Arab–Israeli conflict

The Islamic Republic of Iran's attitude towards the Middle East peace process is a natural outgrowth of revolutionary Iran's political and doctrinal view of the Arab–Israeli conflict. For Iran, the role of Israel as oppressor of the Palestinians has been ideologically congruent with its role as agent of the West and partner to the Shah and thus as historical antagonist to the Iranian republic itself. But the Islamic Republic's attitude towards Israel should not be seen merely in the context of revolutionary or post-revolutionary doctrine: anti-Zionist activism on the part of the Iranian clergy preceded the establishment of the state of Israel, long before Khomeinism appeared as a coherent ideology. The threat of a possible loss of Muslim land and the unique role and status of Jerusalem as a religious symbol to Sunni and Shia alike helped to facilitate political and communal interaction between the clerical leaderships of Iran and Palestine in the 1930s and 1940s. During the 1940s the prominent Iranian cleric and scholar Ayatollah Khorasani actively pursued the defence of Muslim interests in Palestine and developed a close association with the Palestinian Mufti and national leader Haj Amin al-Husseini. (Al-Husseini's strategic interest in reaching out beyond his Sunni constituency was also evidenced in his *fatwa* of 1936 regarding Alawis as 'good Muslims'.) As an echo of Muslim sentiment inside and outside the Arab world, Iran voted against the partition of Palestine in 1947 and Ayatollah Kashani's demonstrations against Israel in Tehran in 1948 helped to set the tone for what was to remain an ambivalent formal and diplomatic relationship with Israel throughout the Pahlavi period despite the emergence of strong ties between the two states under the Shah. The

33

continuing antagonism between the Iranian clergy and the Jewish state was in fact manifest as early as 1962 in Khomeini's very first stirrings against the Shah. Khomeini's speeches before his exile from Iran in 1965 already foreshadow some of the main themes he was later to develop during the struggle for Iran, such as the links between the Shah and Israel, the role of Israel as usurper of Islamic rights in Palestine and the linkage between the Shah, Israel and the United States.

Hostility to Zionism and Israel has thus played a vital role as an instrument of Iranian revolutionary mobilization. Anti-Zionism and hostility to Israel as a state must also be set against the background of the extensive collaboration between the Shah and Israel over three decades. Despite the Shah's officially cautious approach to Iranian–Israeli relations, Israeli support for the Iranian military, and in particular the role of Mossad – the Israeli secret service – in training and cooperating with SAVAK, the Shah's secret police, was widely seen in Iran as incontrovertible evidence of Israel's direct implication in the excesses of the Shah and of the community of interest between the two states. During the period of mass mobilization against the regime, it was therefore not difficult to evoke the image of Israel as an insidious ally of the Shah as well as to emphasize its perceived role in helping to suppress Iran's internal opposition, both religious and secular. The power of such images was not merely rhetorical; it was rooted in the reality of intimate Iranian–Israeli politico-strategic relations as 'partners in oppression', as partners in trade (by the end of the Shah's regime, Israel was receiving 75% of its oil from Iran and Iran was the largest foreign customer for Israeli arms), as active collaborators in support of the Kurdish insurgency against Iraq, and as common enemies of such movements as Arab nationalism/Islamic radicalism, etc. Hostility to Israel and Zionism also provided a focus for galvanizing specifically *Islamic* sentiment against the Shah, especially after 1967 and the Israeli occupation of the whole of Palestine, including Arab Jerusalem. Oppression by the Shah or Israeli agents within Iran itself thus came to be seen as a logical extension of Israeli oppression in the Occupied Territories. The instrumentality of hostility to Israel and Zionism in the struggle against the Shah should thus not be understood as in any way disingenuous. On the contrary, the persistence of anti-Israeli sentiments as a continuing element of Iranian internal and external activism indicates the deep resonance of such slogans, continuing up to the present.

For Khomeini, the defeat and 'removal' of Israel was integral to the ultimate success of the Islamic movement, regionally and, ultimately, globally. As an externally imposed inauthentic manifestation in the area, and the 'illegitimate offspring' of superpower arrogance and hegemonism, Israel would have to be defeated and Jerusalem liberated before the Iranian revolution itself could run its full course. In raw ideological terms, the Khomeinist world-view does not appear to allow much space for the prospect of coexistence between Iran as the prototypical Islamic state and the Islamic movement as a whole on the one hand, and Israel as a separate Jewish polity on the other – although, despite alleged anti-Semitism, Khomeini did not appear to have any intrinsic problem with a non-political Jewish presence within the fold of Islam.

Iran's adoption of the Palestinian cause can also be seen as an important and effective way of reaching into the Arab/Sunni world. On the one hand, by positing the liberation of Palestine as a central Iranian mission, Khomeini emphasized the trans-Islamic bond as a means of transcending both the Arab/Persian and the Sunni/Shiite divides. In contradistinction, this commitment to the Arab/Sunni cause of Palestine also served to assert Islamic Iran's revolutionary credentials as compared with the lassitude of the more conservative Arab states towards Israel, including – eventually – the PLO itself. Indeed, without Iran's formal dedication to the Palestinian cause it is questionable whether its alliance with Syria could have withstood the stresses and strains of the past fifteen years, especially during what was, for Syria, the intensely problematic Iranian pursuit of the war against Iraq after 1982. Iran's pro-Palestinian profile has helped to justify and rationalize Syria's continuing alliance with Iran as well as Iran's own interventions in the Arab–Israeli arena, including its close relationship with radical anti-PLO Palestinian groups and the expeditionary force of Pasdaran deployed in the Bikaa after 1982.

Although there is little to suggest that the Khomeinist view of the struggle with Israel was anything but sincere, Iran's subsequent readiness to deal with Israel as early as 1981 over arms (and later arms for hostages) also suggests that non-ideological and strategic factors can play a role among some sectors of the Iranian leadership in determining policy when necessary. In this context it may be useful to distinguish between the Khomeinist/clerical line within Iranian decision-making and the more institutionalized state apparatus and bureaucracy. During the early 1980s, representatives of the latter may have recognized not only the immediate need for military aid from whatever source was available, but also the importance of *strategic* as opposed to purely doctrinal considerations. From the perspective of Iranian *raison d'état*, as was deftly recognized by the Shah, there may be a desirable balance between

35

maintaining sufficient links with Israel to curb Arab pressures on Iran, and at the same time building a sufficiently solid relationship with at least some of the major Arab centres of power to contain Israeli regional aggrandizement. However, the transactions of 1981–5 did not crystallize into any such general policy and remained largely furtive, intermittent and opportunistic. While strategic considerations (in particular the Iraqi factor) have undoubtedly helped to cement and sustain Iran's relations with Syria, there is no evidence of any erosion in the doctrinal impediments to a truly 'balanced' Iranian relationship with Israel. The early Iranian–Israeli exchanges may now be seen as temporary aberrations rather than any significant breach in Iran's post-revolutionary dogma.

The Iranian position on a political resolution to the Arab–Israeli conflict is based on a number of fundamental assumptions. The most deep-rooted of these is that Israel is intrinsically uninterested in any true peace because it is tyrannical and usurping by its very nature, and will not or cannot contemplate making any real political or territorial concessions to the Palestinian–Arab side. Concessions offered to Israel, such as recognition or peaceful coexistence, are therefore not merely a betrayal of Arab–Muslim historical rights in Palestine but are also illusory and self-defeating, since they only reinforce Israeli intransigence and bellicosity. But even were Israel to reconcile itself to a compromise based on the partition of Palestine, this would not resolve the problem of the Palestinian refugees evicted from their homeland in 1948. A political solution that addressed only the problem of the territories occupied in 1967 would condemn the majority of the Palestinian people who live outside these territories to a perpetual refugee existence. In broad terms, therefore, the Iranian position brooks no political resolution that precludes the restitution of Palestine to its rightful owners and the right of the refugees to return to their homeland. While the Iranian position does not disallow the use of political means in pursuit of this goal, it remains highly sceptical as to the utility of any political effort that is divorced from armed action or the readiness to resort to force.

Iran's political line and its recipe for a solution to the Arab–Israeli conflict should, however, be carefully distinguished from the implications this line entails for Iran itself. Here there appears to be a real divergence of views as to the role of Iran in the struggle for the liberation of Palestine over the past decade and a half. The revolutionary 'Khomeinist' view has traditionally prescribed an all-out Islamic struggle where Iran plays the role of vanguard-prototype and in which the defeat of Israel is but one element of the struggle to establish a universal

Islamic government. This position, most closely associated with the 'radical tendency' in Tehran, has called for an active Iranian operational role in the confrontation with Israel and has support among the clergy and elements of the armed forces including the leadership of the Pasdaran. Its strength has tended to fluctuate with the ebb and flow of the internal struggle in Iran and was initially contained upon the assumption of the presidency by Hojat al-Islam Hashemi Rafsanjani in 1989 after Khomeini's death. The standard official line – at last since the late 1980s – has been most visibly propounded by the Iranian Foreign Ministry and has been generally believed to reflect the view of the 'moderates', including Rafsanjani himself. This line has posited a less direct role for Iran based on the assumption that the main burden of the struggle will/ should be carried by the Palestinians themselves and by the other Arab parties (primarily Syria) that have not yet given up the fight. However, the continuing internal power struggles in Tehran have seen an apparent revival in the influence of the 'radicals' (aided and abetted by Iran's spiritual leader Ayatollah Khamene'i) at the expense of the supporters of President Rafsanjani, but the effect of this on Iran's posture regarding an Arab–Israeli settlement remains uncertain. In broad outline, neither the 'radicals' nor the 'moderates' deny the right of the Palestinians and the Lebanese to continue with their armed resistance to Israeli occupation, nor are there any tangible differences between the two trends as to Iran's readiness to provide moral and material aid to those Palestinian and Lebanese factions that seek it from Tehran. So far, at least, the drift of Rafsanjani's post-Khomeinist pragmatic line has been to move Iran yet further away from any direct action against Israeli targets while maintaining the traditional close ties with groups such as Hizbullah and Islamic Jihad. Whether this will change dramatically as a result of the possible revitalization of the 'radical' tendency or the re-election of a new 'radical' president after 1997 (without the unlikely prospect of a constitutional amendment Rafsanjani himself will be constitutionally ineligible for a third term of office) depends not only on the new internal balance of power within Iran, but equally on the actions and reactions of the external powers that Iran regards as its antagonists, particularly Israel.

Any direct Israeli escalation of the conflict with Iran could well feed the 'radicals' and help to recharge the bases of their internal support. In fact, one of the most salient features of Iran's own posture in the Arab–Israeli arena until now has been its extreme caution in avoiding any direct confrontation with Israel. Besides the limited Pasdaran presence in the Bikaa (which has been reduced by Rafsanjani since 1989–90), there has been little evidence of any significant Iranian participation in anti-Israeli armed activity since the revolution. Regardless of the periodic swings in the internal balance of power in Tehran, Iranian opposition to Israel has not manifested itself in any meaningful military commitment or application of military force. Besides Iran's self-declared mission of providing aid to associated 'radical' and proxy groups, there has been no Iranian propensity to risk an open clash with Israel despite the often strident rhetoric to the contrary. Even when circumstances may have afforded a propitious moment for such Iranian action, Khomeini himself was apparently circumspect in his attitude towards a direct Israeli–Iranian confrontation. According to the testimony of former interior minister Ali Akbar Mohtashemi, Khomeini vetoed the participation of Iranian combat and volunteer forces alongside Syrian forces during the 1982 Israeli invasion of Lebanon. Mohtashemi (then ambassador to Damascus and overseer of Iranian interests in Lebanon) reports Khomeini as arguing that Iran 'could not fight Israel over such long distances and in the absence of common borders with Lebanon and Palestine' and that the war was thus 'the responsibility of the Arabs'. Khomeini also pointed to the problems that Iran could face with Turkey were it to attempt to overfly Turkish territory in order to supply an expeditionary force in Syria. For Khomeini, the utmost priority was the war against Iraq and the installation of an Islamic regime in Baghdad, after which confrontation with Israel could become possible. Khomeini's understanding of the practical and logistical problems facing an Iranian attempt to engage Israel directly still appears to underpin current Iranian policy.

It could be argued that Iran's success in its proxy war via Hizbullah and the Palestinian Islamicists has rendered a strategy of direct confrontation with Israel both unwise and unnecessary and has preserved a careful measure of deniability for Iranian-inspired actions. The paradox, however, is that Iran does not seek such 'deniability', nor does it disguise its deep animosity towards Israel. Far from attempting to distance themselves from anti-Israeli activism, Iran's leaders have made hostility to Israel a defining characteristic of the Islamic Republic itself. The 'war by proxy' therefore has less to do with any perceived need to mask Iran's anti-Israeli commitment and more to do with its realization that there is not much else that can be effectively done to oppose Israel by force. Given the geopolitical realities facing Iran, and setting all ideological considerations aside, few in Tehran harbour many illusions about the limits of Iranian power and the prospects of success for any military endeavour designed to defeat and 'uproot' Israel.

At most, therefore, Iran can be seen as an irritant to Israel via its proxy activities rather than any substantial strategic threat. Having had direct and protracted experience of one of the most brutal and intensive military struggles since the end of the Second World War, the Iranian politico-military establishment must be fully aware of the true nature and requirements of state-to-state warfare in the modern age. Iranian caution must also have been recently reinforced by the – albeit vicarious – demonstration of the effectiveness of high-tech weaponry during Desert Storm.

Iran's attitude towards the military struggle against Israel can be seen in the light of some of the more global characteristics of its foreign policy. In this respect there appears to be a clear dichotomy between Iran's *ideological* and declarative stance and the practical implications this entails for Iranian foreign policy in the field. Iranian relative self-restraint *vis-à-vis* Israel is thus consistent with its policy towards a number of other current conflicts. Even where there has a been a clear *prima facie* case for 'defending Islam' against external aggression, Iran's stance has been muted or largely inert. Iran's position on the Chechen crisis showed an obvious desire to maintain good relations with Russia, despite its onslaught against Iran's Chechenian Muslim brethren. Iran's national interest in stability and security on its northern borders and its need to maintain access to Russian arms and trade, as well as the prospects of new trans-Caucasian oil pipelines, have all weighed against a destabilizing Iranian role in the former Soviet Islamic republics or even a clear condemnation of Russian 'anti-Muslim' actions.

The Iranian response to the plight of Bosnia's Muslims has also been limited despite a stronger declarative stance than over Chechenia. Iran's economic dealings with the Serbs and its material support for the Bosnian war effort reflect some of the factors that underlay its reactions to Chechenia (including the Russian factor) but equally point to the limits of its ability or desire to pursue a truly interventionist international policy.

Iranian self-restraint has also been evident in Central Asia, the Azeri–Armenian conflict, the civil strife in Afghanistan, and most impressively with regard to Saddam's butchery of Iraqi Shiites during the post-Gulf war rebellion in southern Iraq. In all these instances, Iranian foreign policy has effectively suspended its ideological imperative in favour of a rational calculation of state interests.

In the immediate post-revolutionary period and under the influence and inspiration of Ayatollah Khomeini, Iran's revolutionary ideals may have carried within them the seeds of a new regional reconfiguration of power, with Iran playing a potentially significant role as an active anti-

Israeli force. An Iranian–Syrian-Iraqi military alliance, for instance, or a large-scale deployment of Iranian military might to Syria/Lebanon could have posed a serious strategic challenge to Israel. Even if such changes had not led to an all-out confrontation in the area they would almost certainly have had a profound effect on both the Arab and Israeli positions regarding a settlement, including a possibly negative influence on the prospects for a durable Israeli–Egyptian peace. However, the eight years of the Iraqi–Iranian war effectively aborted the emergence of such a new regional balance and put paid to any real chance of a grand Arab–Iranian anti-Israeli war coalition, regardless of whether such a prospect was ever a practical possibility to begin with. In one sense, the Iranian–Syrian alliance can be seen to represent the residual nub of such a grand scheme and the maximum that was realistically attainable in the prevailing circumstances. After the effective defeat of Iran in the war with Iraq, the death of Khomeini further deflated Iran's revolutionary fervour and the natural process of erosion of Iranian activism has been accelerated by the daunting tasks of postwar reconstruction and the ever-pressing needs of the Iranian economy.

The Syrian view of the Arab–Israeli conflict

Pan-Arabism and the Palestine question: Assad's imprint
As the largest front-line Arab power in the Mashriq, Syria's role in the conflict has been partly determined by geopolitics and partly by its own deep-seated self-image and aspirations. Syria's historical ties with Palestine and the emergence of twentieth-century Syrio-centric Arab nationalism have also played a vital role in shaping contemporary Syrian attitudes and in forming the ideological and political underlay of the current Baathist regime. After the 1948 Arab–Israeli war (when the Syrian role was relatively modest) and particularly since the 1950s, successive Syrian regimes have consistently seen Israel as a profound challenge, not only to Syrian national and local interests (e.g. in Lebanon) but to the transnational interests of the Arab nation as a whole. With the advent to power of the Baath party and the adoption of Baathism as the official state ideology in 1963, Syrian nationalism and pan-Arabism have tended to converge as primary influences on Syrian foreign policy generally and on Syria's attitude towards Israel in particular. While the Baath Party itself has undergone significant political and ideological change during the past thirty years of its rule in Syria, the Assad regime

represents important elements of both continuity and change within the context of Syria's recent political and historical heritage.

Over the past quarter of a century, and despite the existence of a substantial party and state apparatus, Syrian decision-making regarding Israel and all other major regional and domestic issues has been decisively influenced by the views and *modus operandi* of President Assad himself. This is not to suggest that the Syrian President's decisions are unencumbered by the views and interests of other elements within Syria's political and institutional establishment, or that he is immune to the pressures of public sentiment even within the relatively controlled Syrian domestic environment. It means, rather, that Assad – especially since the decisive showdown with the Islamic opposition in the early 1980s – has given the Syrian position a measure of authority and credibility unequalled by most other Arab states.

Although Assad's views and outlook represent a retrenchment from the more extreme rejectionist forms of Baathism (as represented by the predecessor regime of Salah Jedid) and have manifested themselves in a unique combination of caution, pragmatism and occasional daring, Assad has never severed himself from his basic ideological roots. From this perspective, the struggle with Israel, although undeniably aggravated by the occupation of Syrian soil on the Golan since 1967, is not to be seen as a purely territorial issue. Insofar as Israel is an alien imposition created and sustained by Western – primarily US – moral and material support, it differs little from the various waves of political, military and cultural Western assaults that the area has been subject to since the Crusades. For Assad himself the Crusader analogy (though currently less in use in his public discourse than previously) has always been powerful and particularly apt, stressing as it does the long-term view and the inexorable rejection by the area of any unnatural implantations within it. The Crusader analogy should also be set against Assad's understanding of Syria's more recent historical experience. In this context, the loss of the Golan appears as part of a process of continuous truncation of the Syrian heartland at the hand of external powers: first with the creation of Greater Lebanon in 1920, then with the British 'invention' of trans-Jordan in 1921, then with the loss of Iskandaroun (Alexandretta) to Turkey in 1939, then with the consolidation of Israel in 'southern Syria' in 1948 etc. For much of its recent history Syria – as it stands within its post-independence borders – has thus seen itself as a relatively artificial construct, more the product of French and British colonial machinations during their respective mandates rather than the culmination of any authentic indigenous process of national formation. This perception partly explains Syria's chronic instability in the 1950s and 1960s, its traditional and 'natural' impulse towards Arab unity and its deep-seated fear of foreign or locally instigated 'plots' aimed at its further dismemberment. Yet while Assad has carried much of this baggage with him over the past quarter of a century, it is important to recognize that his rule has also seen a significant move away from radical pan-Arabism or the notion of a 'greater Syria' towards a more localized 'Syrianism'. In this sense, despite Syria's historical experience and the regime's Baathist underpinnings, the primary driving motivation of Syrian policy under Assad has been directed inwards towards the consolidation of the regime and the expansion of the economy, and outwards towards the defence of Syria as it exists within its standing borders against foreign threats, rather than any active ambitions to redraw Syria's post-independence borders. The only significant exception to this rule concerns Lebanon, where Syria's objectives have occasionally been pursued with an active offensive bent. It nonetheless remains arguable that Syria's Lebanese policy has been both largely reactive in its response to Israeli encroachment and perceived Palestinian or Maronite aggrandizement and also less concerned with the formal incorporation of Lebanon under Syrian rule than with the maintenance of strong Syrian influence and control over the Lebanese arena.

Syrian hostility to Israel is therefore essentially reactive, based on a deep-seated perception of an Israeli military, political and cultural threat. But this hostility also has other elements, primary among them the Syrian commitment to the Palestine cause. From a Baathist pan-Arab perspective, the creation of Israel is not only morally unjust and a trespass against the Palestinians but a transgression against the Arab people and the greater Arab homeland. In this sense, the Syrian/Arab–Israeli conflict is not merely a political confrontation but a clash of destinies and civilizations. Israel is seen as a device to perpetuate Arab division and weakness, thus facilitating the continued external exploitation and manipulation of the Arab world and its resources.

Syria's commitment to the Palestine cause must also be seen in the light of the costs and risks that have marked the conflict with Israel. Syrian forces participated in the 1948 war and in a series of clashes with Israel on the demilitarized zones around Lake Tiberias between 1948 and 1967. After 1967, Syria had to contend with territorial loss on the Golan, and considerable suffering to its civilian population including the evacuation or destruction of around 163 villages and some 150,000 refugees from the Golan area. The 1967, 1973 and 1982 wars saw large-scale military human and material losses (including some 20,000 military casualties killed and wounded) and the gradual mortgaging of the Syrian economy to sustain defence costs. Throughout most of the 1980s military expenditure averaged some 14–16 per cent of Syria's GNP, reaching over 50 per cent of government spending by the end of the decade, seriously affecting the Syrian economy. Although subsequent steps towards economic liberalization and increased oil revenues in the 1990s have lessened the direct economic impact of the confrontation, the Syrian perception of human and material sacrifice for the Palestinian cause remains strong. The result has been a keen feeling that these sacrifices should not be in vain and that Syria itself has a political and moral stake in the shape and nature of a Middle East settlement, one that transcends the Palestinian's own narrow interests and aspirations. Insofar as Baathist doctrine calls for Arab unity and singularity of purpose, and particularly in the light of Syrian–Palestinian historical intimacy, the Palestinians have thus not been accorded the unequivocal right to fully autonomous decision-   making regarding their fate or the future of the conflict with Israel. While accepting the existence of a 'Palestinian people with the right to self-determination' (including statehood), Syria under Assad has consistently argued that Palestine is too vital an issue for Syria itself and too central a pan-Arab concern to be left to the Palestinians (or any other Arab party acting independently) to dispose of alone as they see fit. Indeed, the Syrian Baath, albeit before Assad's assumption of power, can claim to have nurtured and sustained the rebirth of modern Palestinian nationalism through its early patronage of Fateh in the early 1960s. For much of the past two decades, a major point of contention and political friction between Syria and the PLO has centred on the former's refusal to acknowledge the Palestinian 'right to independent decisions' (*Istiqlaliyat al-qarar al-Filastini*).

Syria's dealings with the PLO and its political decisions often appear to smack of manipulation and narrow self-interest. Syria has in fact sought to maintain a strong measure of influence over the Palestinian movement, as during the PLO sojourn in Lebanon between 1970 and 1982, and has intervened forcefully both directly and by proxy against the PLO when it deemed such action necessary (as, for instance, with Mount Lebanon in 1976 and Tripoli in 1983). Syria's attitude towards the PLO can be seen partly as a function of inter-Arab competition and the fear that other Arab parties may gain decisive influence within the movement at Syria's expense, and partly as a reflection of the regional weight and importance of the Palestinian issue *per se*. Syrian rejection of PLO political and diplomatic initiatives such as the 1988 recognition of Israel and the 1993 Oslo deal may have a pan-Arab guise and rationale, but often spring more from Syria's deep fear of a reshaping of the region without due concern for its particular interests. While such fears may be understandable at one level, they also point to Syria's chronic feeling of insecurity and to the very slow-moving nature of its own decision-making process. By and large, Assad's response to sudden initiatives and politico-diplomatic surprises has not been positive, particularly when they are seen to affect Syria's ability to play its own 'Palestinian card'. Yet despite this element of manipulation, the embrace of the Palestinian cause in Syria has been pervasive and has permeated the political, cultural and educational systems at almost every level. In its own eyes, Syria is not only the foremost Arab champion of the Palestinian cause, it also carries a special responsibility for its ultimate fate. No final resolution of this problem can therefore be achieved without Syrian satisfaction as to its terms.

Syria and Israel: the doctrine of 'strategic parity'
Beside the political and ideological roots of Syria's attitude to the Arab–Israeli conflict lie some vital strategic considerations. There is, first, a natural tendency towards competition for regional power and influence between two powerful and geographically contiguous states. Syrian–Israeli rivalries stem not only from the specificity of Syria's adopted message and self-appointed role, but equally from the thrusting encroachment of an alien and dynamic entity on Syria's natural sphere of influence. Secondly, the Syrian perception of a powerful and direct Israeli threat to both Syrian national and pan-Arab security was exacerbated ever since the Arab defeat of 1948 by an ever-widening gap in the balance of power in Israel's favour – up to and including Israel's unsafeguarded and unmatched possession of a nuclear arsenal. The 1967 war put Israeli forces within relatively easy striking distance of Damascus and generally stoked Syrian fears of an aggressive, expansionist Israel bent on the domination and fragmentation of the Syrian-Arab hinterland. After 1967, the Israeli threat was amplified by the developing US–Israeli alliance, the emergence of the United States as the sole advanced arms supplier to Israel, and the apparent Israeli role as proxy guarantor of US 'imperial' interests in the area. The Israeli–US symbiosis also helped to consolidate Syria's own countervailing strategic relationship with the Soviet Union (although it is a measure of Assad's caution that this was

not formalized by treaty until 1980). With the Soviet Union, Syria found a common ideological stance against US and Western imperialism, but perhaps more importantly, a vital political and military counterweight to the opposing superpower and its local clients including Israel and other parties in the region. The need to redress the strategic imbalance created by Israel's 1967 victory and its constantly strengthening ties with the United States remained a central Syrian concern until the early 1990s. Syria's doctrine of 'strategic parity' and its eventual alliance with Iran can also be seen as part of a sustained campaign by Syria to contain or deter Israel, and to create a more favourable strategic environment for itself in the area.

The doctrine of 'strategic parity' was developed in the aftermath of Egypt's defection from the conflict in the late 1970s and was predicated on the assumption that Syria would henceforth have to bear the brunt of any future military showdown with Israel, given its geostrategic position as the major remaining Arab front-line power. In one sense it required a sustained effort to build up and upgrade Syrian military capabilities, including the acquisition of a long-range missile and chemical warhead capability against the Israeli heartland. At another level it required the reinforcement of Syria's political posture and its military deterrent against Israel through the maintenance of close ties with the Soviet Union, its only source of advanced weaponry. Equally, 'parity' required both the maintenance of full control over the situation in Lebanon, Syria's soft underbelly, and the extension of Syria's regional relations and alliances and the development of any potential new points of pressure against Israel to substitute for the loss of Egypt. Given the state of inter-Baath relations and the personal antipathy between Assad and Saddam Hussein, and despite some pro-forma attempts to bring about a Syrian–Iraqi reconciliation, Syria recognized the very limited prospects of a revived 'eastern front' to counter the strategic imbalance in Israel's favour. The two other potential regional partners capable of reinforcing Syria's position were Iran and Saudi Arabia. The Iranian revolution and the developing relations with Iran thus appeared to strengthen Syria's political hand and provide it with a significant corrective to the loss of Egyptian power and influence. At the same time, Syria continued to give special weight to its relations with Saudi Arabia not least because of Saudi financial aid (as sanctioned by the 1978 Baghdad Summit's support for the Syrian-led 'Steadfastness Front') and Saudi political support which helped to legitimize Syria's Lebanon role in the Arab arena – as exemplified by the 1976 Riyadh Summit and the later Taif accords of

1989. Although the Syrian–Saudi connection remained strong throughout the late 1970s and 1980s, Syria's perception of Iran as a potential partner was severely disturbed by the Iraqi invasion of Iran, and its belief in its military capabilities and in the value of the strategic Soviet 'umbrella' was badly shaken by the demonstration of Israeli military high technology over the Bikaa Valley in June 1982. After 1982 Syria continued to make a tremendous effort to develop and modernize its armed forces, but effective 'parity' in the sense of a Syrian-directed war coalition, a credible Soviet protective umbrella or a full-scale unilateral offensive capability (or any combination of the above) became a decreasingly viable prospect. By the late 1980s the final blow to this doctrine was delivered by a combination of Syrian economic weakness, the unbridgeable Israeli technological gap, and Soviet unwillingness to continue to underwrite Syria's grander military ambitions.

Nonetheless, those elements of 'parity' pertaining to Syria's unilateral defensive and deterrent posture, and in particular its long-range missile and chemical warhead capabilities, have remained central to its overall strategic approach to the conflict with Israel. The crux of Syria's current military stance lies in a negative form of 'parity' predicated less on general (or weapon-to-weapon) military equivalence with Israel, and more on a strategic stalemate where Israeli offensive action – even a Syrian military defeat – may be possible, but only at an unacceptable price from an Israeli point of view. In essence 'parity' has been reduced to a Syrian form of containment of Israeli superiority. The ability to raise the cost of Israeli-initiated action beyond the threshold of Israeli acceptability has become the cornerstone of Syria's view of war and peace in the region. Within the context of limited vulnerability to Israel, Syria has thus been able to absorb the generally negative changes in its strategic environment since Camp David and at the same time continue to seek a political solution to the conflict. Syria's perception of its bargaining power and hence its faith in the ultimate viability of the negotiating process is very much a function of its confidence in its deterrent and defensive capabilities and to this end it has continued to seek their enhancement well after the consolidation of the Syrian–Israeli track at Madrid. Given that the Arab–Israeli military confrontation has no real current or foreseeable meaning beyond the possibility of a Syrian–Israeli conflict, Syria's sense of the value of its own military stance has also been heightened. The political price that Syria will seek in return for ending this historical confrontation is thus likely to be high.

1973 and after: the Syrian approach to a settlement

Syria under Assad has in fact long contemplated the possibility of a political resolution of the conflict with Israel. In contrast to the pre-Assad Baathist tendency towards a 'scientific socialism' with emphasis on 'wars of popular liberation' as a means of confronting Israel, Syrian policy under Assad has undergone a process of gradual but continuous pragmatic evolution. As early as 1971 (and again in 1972), Assad signalled his willingness to accept a political solution based on UN Security Council Resolution 242, conditional on a total Israeli withdrawal and the fulfilment of Palestinian rights. For Assad and Sadat the 1973 war was a necessary prelude to achieving an 'honourable' settlement with Israel, whatever its precise terms. By 1974 Assad was willing to take practical steps in this direction. Alongside formal Syrian acceptance of UN Security Council Resolution 338 and its precursor Resolution 242, Assad responded positively to renewed US efforts to mediate in the Middle East. This marked an important change in Syrian policy. First, it clearly indicated Syria's willingness to enter into a sustained diplomatic engagement with the United States despite political and ideological differences between the two sides – a position unaltered in principle by Assad since. Second, it showed Assad's readiness to enter into practical arrangements with Israel on the ground, as exemplified by the 1974 disengagement agreement on the Golan, which has been scrupulously adhered to by Syria for the past two decades. Third, it demonstrated an important characteristic of Assad's decision-making, namely his capacity to pursue Syria's perceived national interest regardless of other potentially inhibiting external factors. In this instance, Syria's very close relationship with the Soviet Union prevented neither Assad's intimate involvement with Henry Kissinger's policies, which were predicated on Soviet exclusion, nor the unprecedented reception of President Nixon in Damascus in June 1974, only a few months after the devastation wrought on Syria by US weapon systems during the October 1973 war.

In the immediate aftermath of the 1973 war, both Egypt and Syria initially followed a similar policy of step-by-step military disengagement, both cooperated extensively with the United States in this regard, and both were publicly committed to the implementation of UN Security Council Resolutions 242/338 on the understanding that this entailed a total evacuation of Arab lands occupied by Israel in 1967. But unlike Sadat, who soon turned almost exclusively to the United States as an active American partner and ally, and ultimately directly to Israel itself, Assad believed that the role of the Soviet Union was indispensable from a Syrian-Arab point of view both as arms supplier and as counterweight to the United States. He also believed that an international conference was necessary for a negotiated settlement to take place.

By the late 1970s Syria was totally immersed in Lebanon and the notion of an international conference, so central to Syria's post-1973 diplomatic posture, had all but disappeared from the US, Israeli and Egyptian agendas. Sadat's visit to Jerusalem in November 1977 and the subsequent Egyptian moves towards a separate peace with Israel dealt a shattering blow to Syria's post-1973 politico-diplomatic strategy and its readiness to cooperate with the United States in the search for a settlement. Syria's sense of an Egyptian betrayal of pan-Arab values was compounded by its feeling of heightened insecurity and US prevarication. From a Syrian point of view, the US devotion to the success of the Egyptian–Israeli talks came at the expense of its professed interest in a more comprehensive settlement, and effectively highlighted America's unwillingness or inability to reach out beyond its policy of partial and dangerously destabilizing separate Arab–Israeli agreements. With the advent of the Reagan administration, the US view of Syria as a Soviet surrogate all but destroyed the prospects for any renewed US–Syrian understanding which had been briefly glimpsed under President Carter. As the Reagan administration's politico-ideological and 'strategic' affinity with the Likud government developed, the dominant approach in the United States and Israel during much of the 1980s centred on ensuring the exclusion of Syria from the process rather than any serious attempt to re-engage its interest in a settlement. The main thrust of Syrian policy throughout this period was largely defensive: until well into the 1980s, Syria's first objective was to prevent any further Arab defections along the lines of Sadat's. The attempt to nourish a 'radical' Arab collective response via the 'Steadfastness Front', the brief rapprochement with Iraq (in 1978–9) the high-risk involvement in Lebanon, the occasional escalation of tension with Jordan (as in 1980), the continuous friction with the PLO and the alliance with Iran, all reflected this dominant concern. Parallel to this was a Syrian determination not to submit to any US–Israeli diktat regarding a settlement. Syria's readiness to confront the United States in Lebanon after 1982 was meant to signify its resistance to direct US intrusion into its backyard and emphasize the inadvisability of attempting to reconfigure the area against Syria's will. But despite US–Syrian tensions, Assad never lost sight of the fact that the United States was the leading external peacemaker in the Middle East. Above all, and up until the Madrid conference of 1991, Syria sought to achieve US and

Israeli recognition of its regional weight and status as a precondition for facilitating the Arab–Israeli peace process. Its main message thus remained constant: the Middle East peace process can move forward only with Syrian consent; without it there can be no prospect of a lasting settlement.

The Fahd Plan, the Reagan Plan and the Fez summits

Syria's position at the outset of the Madrid peace process can be best understood by tracing the development of Syrian policy towards a settlement since the eve of the Israeli invasion of Lebanon in 1982. The decade 1981–91 witnessed some important milestones on the road to Madrid which also afford a useful means by which Syria's position can be compared and contrasted to that of its ally during this period, the Islamic Republic of Iran. While there emerges a measure of overlap and interaction between the two allies, Syrian and Iranian positions on the various proposals for a Middle East settlement between the Fahd Plan/Fez summits of 1981–2 and the Madrid conference of 1991 appear to reflect more the respective national interests and policy objectives of each side separately rather than any fixed common goal or purpose.

In the immediate aftermath of the Israeli invasion of 1982, the United States perceived a window of opportunity to build on the then apparent Israeli success in defeating both the PLO and Syria in Lebanon. The result was the first serious US attempt to set up a framework for a comprehensive Middle East settlement since the Camp David accords of 1979. The Reagan Plan announced on 1 September 1982, only days after the PLO evacuation of Beirut but before the Sabra-Shatilla massacres, reaffirmed the US commitment to Camp David but added important new components regarding the final status of the West Bank and Gaza. For the first time the United States went on record in opposition to both an independent Palestinian state and Israeli annexation, and in support of some form of association between the West Bank and Gaza and Jordan.

Prompted by some early over-optimistic Israeli assessments of Palestinian readiness to break free of Syria and go for the Jordanian option, the Reagan initiative was aimed primarily at Jordan and the Palestinians. At this juncture, the US attitude towards Syria was dominated by Cold War considerations. In line with the Reagan administration's by then well-established politico-ideological antipathy towards Syria as a 'Soviet surrogate', and on the premise that the Israeli invasion of Lebanon had significantly reduced the Syrian–Soviet ability to obstruct any movement towards a settlement, Syria was cut out of the process altogether. Thus Assad was not consulted by the United States prior to the announcement of the new initiative, nor were Syrian concerns addressed by its terms; and not one word appeared in the plan concerning the future of the Israeli occupation of the Golan. To Syria, the Reagan Plan appeared to aim at the completion of the 'Camp David conspiracy' by going yet another step towards a new separate Arab–Israeli deal to be foisted on the Palestinians by a weakened and defeatist PLO in conjunction with an ever-opportunistic King Hussein. The right of the Palestinians to their independent national state was denied by the United States, which continued to ignore UN Resolutions as well as 'ideas of the majority of the world's states' (as common Syrian parlance had it) on this issue. And yet the initial Syrian response to the Reagan Plan was studied and cautious and carefully amounted to less than all-out repudiation. While Israel's early rejection of the plan made it both tactically unsound and unnecessary for Syria to commit itself in a similar manner, Syria was acutely aware of both its own limitations in the immediate aftermath of the Lebanon war and the general Arab mood emerging from it. In fact, in tandem with the Reagan Plan, the Lebanon war had spurred the majority 'moderate' Arab bloc (including Saudi Arabia, Morocco, the PLO, Jordan and – at that stage – Iraq) to call for a collective Arab response to the question of a settlement with Israel. With this in mind, an Arab summit was called to meet at Fez in Morocco in mid-September 1982, shortly after the Reagan initiative was announced.

A number of crucial decisions were made at Fez. A broad Arab consensus was set out for a political settlement with Israel that incorporated both a statement of principles and a general programme for action. For the first time since 1948 the Arab states collectively and formally accepted the partition of Palestine and by extension the existence of Israel, providing that (a) Israel withdrew from all the territories occupied in 1967; (b) all settlements on these territories were dismantled; and (c) a Palestinian state would be established with East Jerusalem as its capital. In return, the Arab states would accept a transitional arrangement for the West Bank and Gaza under UN trusteeship pending the completion of the Israeli withdrawal and, most significantly, a UN Security Council 'guarantee [of] peace for all states in the region including an independent Palestinian state'. Syria's espousal of these of terms for a settlement in September 1982 can be compared and contrasted with its sharp rejection of a very similar set of terms for a settlement with Israel only months earlier. In November 1981, at PLO instigation, Saudi Crown

Prince Fahd had pushed hard for an Arab summit – also to be held at Fez – for the adoption of what was mooted as the 'Fahd Plan'. This plan's importance stemmed not only from the nature of the proposal itself but also from the fact of its adoption by a leading moderate Arab power known until then for its diplomatic reticence as well as its close ties to the United States. The plan suggested a land-for-peace deal with Israel and the setting up of an independent Palestinian state as the basis for ending the Arab–Israeli conflict. Although Syria had been consulted by the Saudis prior to the convocation of the summit, Assad very deliberately sabotaged the meeting by announcing his decision not to attend just a few hours before its first session was due to convene.

There would appear to be little doubt that the Israeli invasion of Lebanon facilitated Syria's responsiveness to Fez-2 as opposed to the abortive 1981 summit. In the first instance, the Fahd Plan was seen by Syria largely as a PLO attempt to outflank it via the Saudis, in possible connivance with the United States. With the PLO very much still within Syria's direct sphere of influence in the Lebanon, the notion of an 'independent' Palestinian decision or initiative on this scale (albeit at one step removed) was unacceptable to Assad almost as a matter of principle. At the same time Assad may have felt that he would come under pressure from the other Arab parties at the summit regarding his nascent relationship with Iran. Given the Syrian interest in nourishing this relationship and the high hopes still maintained by Syria regarding the strategic implications of the Iranian revolution, Assad's reluctance to antagonize Iran or diminish the effect of his Iranian card as a means of leverage in the inter-Arab domain is understandable. Equally, Syria's confidence in its ability to impress its regional weight on all interested parties and to extract a price for its rejectionism (e.g. increased aid from the Gulf states) was still relatively undented in 1981. In the immediate aftermath of the Lebanon war, much of this had changed. For one thing, the eviction of the PLO from Lebanon had paradoxically freed it from its fears of direct Syrian tutelage. More importantly, Syria could now fold its position into that of a collective Arab response to the Reagan Plan rather than any unilateral Arab initiative. Fez-2 was thus portrayed by Syria as a necessary pan-Arab reaction to the unacceptable terms being set out by the United States for a settlement, and moreover one that came in the wake of a lone Syrian stance against the full weight of the Israeli military machine. The Lebanese war of June 1982 had demonstrated conclusively that neither the Arab states nor the Soviet Union (ostensibly Syria's strategic ally) were willing to provide or capable of providing any effective support for Syria when under direct military threat from Israel. A declared readiness to seek a 'just' solution within the prevailing Arab consensus while concurrently seeking to enhance both Syria's defensive capability and its negotiating posture through the attainment of 'strategic parity' with Israel were thus seen as Assad's best options after June 1982. Thus Syria's acceptance of Fez-2 as opposed to its rejection of the 1981 Fahd Plan had less to do with the content of the respective peace proposals and more with their perceived political and strategic context.

Iran's responses to the Fahd initiative, the Reagan Plan and the Fez-2 resolutions are instructive as case studies of its reactions to developments in the peace process and its relations with Syria. Its ideological condemnation of all three initiatives was robust and unequivocal. The Fahd initiative was attacked both as a matter of principle and as an expression of the ill-will of those who devised and supported it. For the Iranians, the initiative was a clear-cut betrayal by dint of its indirect recognition of Israel, the 'Zionist enemy'. At another level, the response was carefully channelled in support of Iranian foreign policy objectives. Reflecting intense Saudi–Iranian Islamic competition as well as differences over the Iran–Iraq war, the plan afforded Iran an important opportunity to flex its muscles in the Gulf and put pressure on Saudi Arabia. It was thus pointedly attacked as a Saudi betrayal of *Islam*.

When the first Fez summit collapsed in disarray Iran seemed happy to claim credit for the derailment of the Fahd Plan. The Iranian foreign ministry issued a statement saying that Iran 'considers the failure of the Arab summit a great victory for the Islamic community and the uncompromising combatants of Palestine' and a 'humiliating setback for the puppet heads of state who embarked on a deal with Zionism'. Rafsanjani, then speaker of the Iranian parliament, the Majlis, went one step further and credited the failure of the initiative to Khomeini's direct intervention and his warnings against the betrayal of Islam. Interestingly, however, he took to task the leaders of the Islamic Arab countries for failing to propose a counter-plan that would 'save the Palestinian refugees', and called for military mobilization by these countries; he did not, however, specify the nature of Iran's own contribution to this force.

The Fahd Plan represented the first potentially substantive development in the Arab–Israeli peace process since the Iranian revolution. Although the Syrian–Iranian alliance was not yet formalized, the plan presented some common – but not necessarily identical – causes for concern. While Syria was not as inimical as Iran to the idea of a settlement, neither party felt compelled at that juncture to applaud an initiative that was not principally designed or initiated to cater for their ideological proclivities or political interests. For both Syria and Iran, the Fahd Plan was a political and ideological challenge in so far as it threatened to weaken their respective hands by forcing the pace and nature of a settlement with Israel or by strengthening other regional actors, such as Saudi Arabia and the PLO, at their expense. The perception of US collusion in the plan also fed both Syrian and Iranian suspicions as to its provenance and purpose. The Iranian attitude to the Fahd Plan was undoubtedly coloured by Syria's reticence and ultimate sabotage of the initiative; but while Iranian rejectionism may have been fired by Syria's negative response, neither country's attitude to the plan can be attributed primarily to the other.

The interaction between the two parties can be seen in a somewhat clearer light after the Reagan Plan and Fez-2. Iran's ideological stance was again unyielding. Before the actual summit was convened, Khomeini once more warned the Arab parties against adopting the Reagan Plan, and suggested that Iran might 'punish' those Gulf countries that did so. The Iranian foreign ministry attacked the summit as 'still bearing the stain of the previous year's [Fahd plan] conspiracy to recognize the Zionist regime'. The Islamic and progressive countries were urged to 'end the life of the Zionist regime in a *Jihad*'. For Iran, the mere inclusion of the Reagan Plan on the agenda of the Arab summit was a 'great deviation from the dreams of the Palestinians'. And yet the Iranian criticism of Fez-2 was relatively restrained compared with its all-out onslaught on the Fahd Plan the year before. As with Fahd, Iran escalated its verbal attacks on the targets it felt were most vulnerable, particularly Saudi Arabia and the Gulf states, but it is noticeable that it did not directly attack Syria for adhering to the summit resolutions, preferring to couch its criticisms of those who did in general terms. Only days after Fez, the massacre of Palestinians at Sabra and Shatila in Lebanon provided the Iranian foreign ministry with the perfect riposte: 'The Zionist regime, following its strategy of occupying the lands between the Nile and the Euphrates, does not stop for a moment, and compromising efforts like the Fez conference will always be answered by such replies [i.e. the massacre of Palestinians] by Zionism.' Nonetheless, in contrast to the calls for Fahd's 'execution' in November 1981, Iran took a distinctly low-key public stance against Syria and its leadership in September 1982.

Iran's view of the Fahd initiative appears in fact to have been substantially different from that of Fez-2. Iranian opposition to Fez-1 was unproblematic and cost-free, since it tallied nicely with Syria's own hostile response. By the time of Fez-2, the Syrian–Iranian alliance that grew out of the March 1982 economic and military accords confronted Iran with a more difficult choice. Total quiescence before the dramatic developments at Fez was politically and ideologically impossible. Yet unrestrained attacks on Syria could destroy the delicate bilateral relations between the two states and hence lose Iran its only significant ally in the Arab world as well as its vital point of access into Lebanon. But perhaps even more importantly, the Arab summit at Fez was a potential opportunity for an Assad–Saddam reconciliation. In the context of the then aggressive Iranian pursuit of the war into Iraqi territory, the political and strategic costs of a falling-out with Syria would have been high. Indeed, and in a possible indirect message to Iran, Assad did meet briefly with Saddam at Fez, albeit with no tangible result. Iran's dilemma comes through in its detailed reaction to the Fez summit resolutions. The Iranian foreign ministry's immediate condemnation of the Arab stance on Israel was matched by the conspicuous absence of any reference to another unanimous resolution supported by Syria on the Iraq–Iran war. In a clear reference to Iran, this resolution committed the summit participants 'to defend all Arab territories and to consider any aggression against any Arab country as an aggression against all the Arab countries'. The summit equally called on all states not to encourage the continuation of the war. The Iranian attack on the Arab position on Israel could be generalized without any direct reference to Syria or any undue negative effect on the relationship between the two countries. But to point out Syrian compliance in a specifically anti-Iranian resolution could have been embarrassing within Iran, as well as an imprudent 'cornering' of Syria itself. Iran's reactions to Fez were thus ultimately pragmatic and in its own self-interest.

Nonetheless, Iran's restraint does not seem to have been taken for granted by Syria. With the evident objective of assuaging Iranian fears and reinforcing Syria's interest in maintaining the alliance, Assad dispatched Ahmad Iskandar Ahmad, Syria's information minister, as his personal envoy to Tehran to 'convey to the Islamic revolution[ary] leadership in Tehran our viewpoints regarding the work and results of the [Fez] conference'. In Tehran Ahmad stressed Syria's support for the Islamic revolution against its 'internal and external enemies' and the strength of the relationship between the two countries, as well as their 'identical viewpoints' regarding Fez and its agenda. Privately, Ahmad pointed out to his Iranian interlocutors that they should not be overly concerned at Syria's acceptance of the Fez resolutions since Syria was convinced that nothing would come of them anyway, and that Syria's participation in the summit was necessary to prevent other Arab parties from offering Israel further concessions. In public, and in a touch of hyperbole probably meant to reassure the Iranians as to Syrian commitment to the relationship, Ahmad asserted that Syria 'consider[s] the Iranian revolution the most important event in the second half of the twentieth century'. In a concise summation of the Syrian assessment of the significance of the Iranian revolution, Ahmad added that it 'has turned the Iranian people and capabilities from an alliance with Israel and from enemies into an alliance with the Arabs struggling with us against Zionism and US imperialism for the liberation of holy Jerusalem'. Catering for Iranian sensitivities, Ahmad also publicly dismissed the brief encounter between Assad and Saddam as of no political significance or content, and directly aligned Syria with Iran against Iraq by stressing the fundamental clash of interests between the two Baathist regimes: 'We are in a conflict with the Iraqi regime. That regime hopes for our removal and we certainly hope for its removal as soon as possible.'

The 1985 PLO–Jordan agreement

Both Fez-2 and the Reagan Plan foundered as a result of a combination of Israeli obduracy and US preoccupation with events in the Lebanon. Besides the ill-fated May 1983 accord between Israel and Lebanon, little of substance was to emerge in terms of progress towards an Arab–Israeli settlement until February 1985 and the agreement between Jordan and the PLO to form a joint delegation to any future international conference on the Middle East – an agreement that collapsed in mutual PLO–Jordanian acrimony in February 1986, one year after its inception.

Syrian opposition to the PLO–Jordan agreement was evident from the start. The agreement appeared to presage yet another US attempt to set up a seperate Arab–Israeli deal at Syria's expense. Neither Egyptian support for the agreement nor the escalating PLO–Syrian conflict in Lebanon (the Beruit 'war of the camps' had started in earnest by mid-1985) inspired Syria to feel positively inclined towards a process that held nothing for Syria itself. Jordan was accused of seeking to complete the 'capitulatory' Camp David accords and of working in collusion with the 'Arafat clique' to rob the PLO of its international status by replacing the organization with Palestinian figures 'chosen by the Jordanian regime'. In fact, Syrian concerns centred not only on the possibility of a separate

PLO–Jordanian deal but also on the prospect of Jordanian 'hegemony' over Palestinian decision-making, indeed over the future of Palestine itself. The idea of a Palestinian–Jordanian confederation (privately described by the Jordanians as 'closer to federation' in their bilateral dealings with the United States) was never favoured by Syria, given its interest in having a determining say in a Palestinian settlement and its apprehensions regarding an Israeli-Jordanian-Palestinian axis along its southern flank. Syrian concerns also encompassed the possible emergence of an Egyptian-Jordanian-Iraqi link, given the close ties between all three parties and Egyptian President Mubarak's active diplomacy on Iraq's behalf.

Throughout 1985 Syria sought to stave off what it perceived as a concerted effort to weaken its position on a Middle East settlement. Although the eventual collapse of the PLO–Jordan agreement cannot be attributed to Syrian pressure alone, Jordan's enthusiasm for a partnership with the PLO was dampened and its freedom of action severely circumscribed by Syria's adamant opposition. The net result of the whole episode was a paradoxical improvement in Jordanian–Syrian relations and a renewed period of stagnation in the peace process.

The PLO–Jordan agreement was the occasion for an almost complete convergence of views between Tehran and Damascus. Unlike Fez-2, there was no apparent cause for discord between the two parties. Upon its announcement, Tehran denounced the agreement as 'a mourning ceremony for the Palestinian cause' and accused the PLO of accepting UN Resolution 242 as a prelude to surrender to Israel. Subsequently Iranian President Khamene'i also wrote to President Assad agreeing on the need to 'combat Israeli aggression and attempts to generalize the Camp David process'. Iran's receptiveness to anti-PLO sentiment was underlined by its formal recognition of the Damascus-based 'Salvation Front' and the visit to Tehran in August 1985 by a delegation from the Front headed by Fateh splinter-group leader Abu Musa. Received by the Iranian Prime Minister Hussein Mosavi, Abu Musa reported that the Iranian leader had condemned Arafat as a 'danger not only to the Palestinian People but to all Islamic liberation movements'. Foremost in Iran's mind, however, was the war with Iraq and the escalating Iraqi aerial campaign against Iranian cities and oil terminals, which was having a devastating effect on the economy. Iranian diplomacy was thus urgently engaged in extending its regional contacts and consolidating its system of alliances and understandings against Iraq. To this end, Syria had succeeded in mobilizing Libyan support for Iran at a trilateral foreign ministerial conference in Tehran in January 1985 and at a follow-up meeting in Damascus, including South Yemen, in March. Given Iran's ideological and political stance on the Arab–Israeli conflict and its immediate preoccupation with the war with Iraq, its readiness to toe the Syrian line on the PLO–Jordan agreement is understandable. But its willingness to make its own independent deals was also to become evident. By the summer of 1985, Iran had embarked on its clandestine 'arms for hostages' projects with Israel and the United States, making clear its ability to discard ideological strictures when necessary in favour of national interest.

For Iran, there was no real need to go beyond Syrian opposition to the PLO–Jordan agreement, given the evident priority that Syria itself attached to this and the broader range of measures at Syria's disposal for putting pressure on the various parties concerned. Indeed, Iran could play a relatively secondary role, echoing Syria's political stance and highlighting its support for groups already within the Syrian orbit such as the Palestinian 'Salvation Front'. Iranian support for Syria was needed not only in the confrontation with Israel, but as a counterbalance to Iraq and a lever against Egypt and Jordan; it was therefore less effective as a means of actively disrupting the agreement (in fact, Iran's allies in Lebanon, Hizbullah, were acting to relieve Syrian pressure on Arafat in the 'war of the camps') and more significant as a component of Syria's overall regional power and influence in facing down the agreement's ramifications. Iran's reward lay in Syria's continuous efforts to maintain pressure on Iraq, and in its role as a buffer against Iran's total regional isolation via contact with Libya and South Yemen.

Iran's general deference to the Syrian line on an Arab–Israeli settlement was reaffirmed at the next crucial juncture in the process. The outbreak of the Palestinian *intifada* in Gaza and the West Bank in December 1987 appeared to wrest the initiative from Damascus and restore much of the PLO's ability to project itself as a central player in the arena. After yet another attempt at a direct bilateral agreement with Israel in April 1987 (the so-called Peres–Hussein London accord), Jordan decided on a 'final' administrative and legal disengagement from the West Bank in mid-1988. Jordan's decision appeared to remove the Kingdom from the Palestinian–Israeli arena, but Syria's interest in attempting to coopt Jordan or prevent it from pursuing a separate policy towards the PLO or Israel remained. Concurrently, the end of the Iran–Iraq war on humiliating terms for Iran left Syria's main regional ally in a much weakened position, undermining Syria's broader notion of 'parity' and its ability to turn its ties with Iran to its own regional advantage. Saddam's prestige and power, by comparison, had never appeared higher.

The 1988 Palestine National Council

US efforts to jump-start the peace process in the wake of the *intifada* once again reached a dead end with a largely negative response from the local parties (with the exception of Egypt) to the Schultz initiative of March 1988. By that autumn, however, there were indicators of a potential change in US policy towards the PLO, were the latter to come out unequivocally in support of UN Security Council Resolution 242 and Israel's right to exist. The tempting prospect of international (i.e. US) legitimation, combined with pressure from the leadership within the Occupied Territories to capitalize on the *intifada*'s gains, finally gave the PLO the courage to take the plunge. At the 19th session of the Palestine National Council (PNC) convened in Algiers in November 1988, Arafat and the Fateh leadership pushed through a series of resolutions establishing an independent Palestinian state and accepting Israel's right to exist by a belated adoption of the 1947 UN partition plan for Palestine. The PNC also put forward a peace plan based on a qualified acceptance of Resolution 242, the withdrawal of Israel from all territories occupied in the 1967 war, the dismantlement of Israeli settlements in the West Bank and Gaza, and the establishment of Arab East Jerusalem as the capital of the Palestinan state, all within the general terms of Fez-2.

In terms of the PLO's historical stance towards Israel, the PNC resolutions marked a sea-change in attitude and a new political maturity. Belated as it was, the formal adoption of the principle of partition and the two-state solution put Israel on the political and moral defensive and gave some credibility to the PLO's claim to a seat at the negotiating table. In December 1988, Chairman Arafat's address to a specially convened UN General Assembly meeting in Geneva ironed out the ambiguities in the PNC's statements regarding Resolution 242 and was deemed sufficiently unequivocal to merit the reward of a US retraction of the 1975 ban on talks with the PLO and the initiation of a formal, authorized US–PLO dialogue in Tunis.

These dramatic changes were received with varying degrees of caution in Damascus and Tehran. For Syria, the right of the Palestinians to establish their own independent state was uncontested and was formally reasserted in a number of official Syrian statements; and given that the PLO's 'peace plan' deviated little from the Fez-2 resolutions accepted by Syria itself, there was little that Syria could fault in the general tenor of the Palestinian initiative. Salvation Front leaders, however, were quoted as criticizing the PNC's acceptance of Resolution 242 on the grounds that this constituted a 'relinquishment of Palestinian national and inalienable rights'. From a similar perspective Iran was strongly critical of the PLO's position on 242 while carefully avoiding a principled stance against the Palestinian state *per se*. In a detailed and authoritative statement by deputy foreign minister Hussein Sheikhul-islam, Iran made clear its distinction between a Palestinian state that would constitute a step towards the liberation of all Palestinian soil and one that would be contingent on the recognition of Israel. While the first was to be supported and lauded, the second would be contrary to the interests and inalienable rights of the Palestinian nation and the Islamic world. Syria's and Iran's virtual identity of views on the PNC was repeated without much nuance with regard to the US–PLO dialogue. Syria's response was to castigate the PLO leadership for making additional concessions and to suggest that the way forward was not through 'begging solutions from others' but through the creation of strategic parity to 'take peace by force'. In a comment on Arafat's Geneva declarations President Khamene'i of Iran rejected the partition of Palestine as unacceptable and called for Zionism to be fought with force. But despite the heightened anti-Arafat rhetoric from Damascus, Tehran and the rejectionist groups, Syrian and Iranian reactions once again were relatively limited and contained. Notwithstanding some claims to the contrary, the murky story of the bombing of Pan Am flight 103 over Lockerbie in December 1988 has not yet generated any credible evidence to suggest an Iranian-rejectionist attempt to derail the peace process, and in any case was evidently not part of any sustained campaign to that end.

Both Syria and Iran appear to have looked elsewhere for a response to these developments. Syria's main concern appears to have been directed towards a possible shift in the Arab balance of power in favour of the Arab 'moderates', now tacitly including Saddam. Syria thus quickly moved to restore its relations with Egypt, which had remained severed since 1979. In this sense Syria's concern was more strategic than tactical. Not opposed to a settlement in principle, Syria's efforts were directed – as always – towards preventing a deterioration of the overall regional balance and the possibility of separate Arab deals with Israel that would weaken its power and negotiating stance. Iran's response, by comparison, was largely tactical. Not itself a player in the peace process, it primarily sought to maintain and develop its ties among the forces most closely associated with its ideological and political line. Thus in December 1988, Iranian leaders (including Khomeini) received Fathi Shiqqaqi, the leader of the Palestinian Islamic Jihad organization, in Tehran for the first time, after his deportation from Gaza by Israel. This visit marked the first real attempt by Iran to develop a direct relationship with Palestinian factions operating inside the occupied territories, a policy subsequently extended to Hamas in 1990. Iran could now claim to have gone beyond Hizbullah and its Shiite base in Lebanon towards some modest but not insignificant relationship with the Islamicist Sunni movement in Palestine.

Desert Storm and after

The Bush administration's focus on a Middle East settlement was evident from its inauguration: Secretary of State James Baker's public rejection of the 'unrealistic vision of a greater Israel' appeared to herald a new and even-handed approach to the conflict in contrast to Reagan's consistently pro-Israeli line. However, by summer 1990 Baker's initiative had finally come to naught. The Iraqi invasion of Kuwait in August 1990 was to be the eventual catalyst for its rebirth.

The first and most important station in the peace process after Operation Desert Storm was President Bush's address to a joint session of Congress in March 1991, in which he spoke explicitly of the need to secure the twin principles of security for Israel and 'legitimate Palestinian political rights'. The United States was set on capitalizing on the postwar regional environment in order to push for a settlement on a scale unseen since the Kissinger shuttles of 1973–4. This time the United States made special efforts to engage Syria and to build on the relationship that had emerged out of the second Gulf war. In June 1991 Bush sent letters to Israeli Prime Minister Shamir, Presidents Assad and Mubarak, and Kings Hussein and Fahd calling for a peace conference in the autumn. The first positive reply came from Damascus, followed by acceptances from the other Arab parties, and eventually – under pressure – from Shamir himself.

Syria's decision to accept the US invitation to the Madrid Conference in July 1991 before a positive response from Israel was a turning-point in the whole process. By coming out first in support of this conference Syria not only embarrassed the Shamir government but gave active succour to the by now massive US political and psychological investment in a general Middle East settlement. More specifically, it reflected Assad's desire to build on the new momentum in Syrian–US relations that had developed out of Syria's positive role in the US-led coalition against

Iraq. In contrast to the policy of ostracism and exclusion pursued by the Reagan administration, the new approach of President Bush and Secretary of State Baker augured well from a Syrian point of view. This approach not only appeared actively to court Syria and recognize its regional role and concerns, but, equally vitally, it stressed the formula of 'land for peace', which was seen in Damascus both as a precondition for Syrian–Arab participation in the peace process and as an indication of US good faith. President Bush's reiteration of this formula in March 1991 also stood in sharp contrast to the Likud government's unyielding dedication to the 'peace for peace' formulation that effectively denied the notion of an Israeli withdrawal from any of the territories occupied in 1967; the scene thus appeared set for a possibly critical divergence of views between Israel and the United States that could be turned to Syrian/Arab advantage. Finally, there was the reality of Syria's limited margins of manoeuvre, given the rapidly diminishing power and capabilities of the Soviet Union and the new post-Gulf war political environment in the Middle East itself.

The main elements of Syria's position on a settlement did not change much between 1973 and 1991 and indeed still hold true. On the eve of the Madrid conference it could be best summarized as follows. First, by recognizing UN Resolutions 242 and 338 Syria had long accepted the reality of Israel, even though it may continue to question its moral and ideological foundations. Second, an Arab–Israeli settlement must be comprehensive in a number of senses: it must be acceptable to all the Arab parties concerned, and should not favour some at the expense of others; and it should address all outstanding issues (on the basis of Resolutions 242 and 338) and not be selective or preferential in its interpretation of the basis for peace. In this context, the Palestinian dimension of a settlement has unique status for Syria. Unlike some Arab parties (e.g. Sadat), Syria rejects any decoupling of Syrian and Palestinian interests for historical, ideological, cultural and strategic reasons. Other factors must therefore be taken into account by the United States and Israel (and consequently all other interested parties) if a truly lasting and stable settlement is to be achieved. The primacy of Syria's interests in Lebanon, and its right to act in defence of these interests, must be recognized. Second, Syria must be acknowledged as a major Arab power with a particular role and standing in the Mashriq. In the Middle East as a whole Syria expects to be treated by Israel and the United States on an equal footing with other regional powers such as Egypt, Iran, Turkey and Saudi Arabia, and eventually Iraq, pending its rehabilitation. In practice this means an end to US or Israeli policies designed to challenge, defeat, exclude or isolate Syria as in the period 1975–90. Within the framework of a process that incorporates all the above elements, Syria is willing to commit itself to a 'strategic decision' for peace and to enter into negotiations with Israel to this end alongside the other Arab parties represented at Madrid.

Iran's public response to Syria's decision to accept the US proposals for a Middle East peace conference for Madrid was unfavourable. Avoiding any direct criticism of the Syrian leadership, Iranian commentaries stressed that Syria's 'accommodation of the [US] plan comforts US imperialism and hegemonism in the region and weakens the sacred cause of Muslim Palestine'. But it is unlikely that the Syrian decision was a total surprise from the Iranian point of view since it had followed a visit to Damascus by President Rafsanjani only one month earlier, and the decision may have been already anticipated and absorbed in Tehran. Syria's eventual attendance in Madrid in late October 1991 saw a similar Iranian response, preceded by a similar effort at Syrian consultation. One month before Madrid, Syrian Chief of Staff Hikmat Shihabi paid an extended visit to Tehran at the head of a high-level delegation. The visit was prompted by Syria's (eventually successful) attempt to push Iran into a more active commitment to release all remaining Western hostages in Lebanon and covered issues of military cooperation as well as questions arising from the peace process and matters of Gulf security. Shihabi also went out of his way to stress publicly the importance of the relationship between the two countries and their understanding of the need for a just and lasting peace 'which will ensure the rights of the Palestinians and return of all occupied territories'.

However, in an effort to draw a line between its tolerance of Syria's position on Madrid and its own political and ideological commitments, Iran organized a 'counter-Madrid' conference in Tehran in late October. This 'International Conference in Support of the Islamic Revolution in Palestine' was attended by Palestinian rejectionists such as Ahmad Jibril's PFLP-GC and included representatives from Islamic Jihad and other Arab Islamicists from Lebanon, Algeria and Sudan as well as opposition groups from all over the Third World. The organization set up a $20 million fund supported by the Iranian Majlis to give succour to the Palestinian people under occupation and help escalate the *intifada*. Addressing the conference, President Rafsanjani declared that Iran was 'even ready to dispatch troops to fight Israel along with the Palestinians'; he made no specific reference to Syria or Syrian policy. Other Iranian speakers such as Ayatollah Khamene'i and former interior minister Mohtashemi were more forceful in their denunciation of the Madrid participants, the latter describing Madrid as 'a declaration of war on Islam and the Muslims'. One measure of the steadfastness of the Syrian–Iranian alliance, however, was that only a few weeks after Madrid, an Iranian Majlis delegation headed by deputy speaker Hussein Hashimian visited Damascus and discussed 'the most important current issues in the Middle East' and both the Tehran and Madrid conferences with no apparent acrimony between the two sides. The talks emphasized Syrian–Iranian ties and the 'need to work continuously to develop and promote them in the interest of the two countries' causes'.

Nevertheless, on the surface at least, after Madrid the divergence between Syria and Iran had become larger and more substantial than ever before. Syria had formally become an active participant in an Arab–Israeli peace process under the direct aegis of the United States and had taken on a new Gulf role exclusive of Iran. But Iranian–Syrian differences on this, as on other issues, have had no substantive effect on their alliance. In fact, the pattern of Iranian reactions and responses to developments in the peace process can be seen to have been consistent all along. Since 1981, Syria and Iran had found common cause in opposing the Fahd initiative, the PLO–Jordan agreement and the PNC's 1988 resolutions, and there was little reason for conflict or tension between them. Where Syria took a line that conflicted with Iran, as towards the second Fez summit and the Madrid conference, Iranian objections to Syrian decisions were indirect and largely unofficial and were deflected towards other targets, such as the PLO, Jordan or Saudi Arabia. Iranian rhetoric notwithstanding, Syrian participation in the peace process was thus dictated by Syria's own national interests and the conviction that Iran's opposition would have no real effect on Syrian policy, or indeed on the durability of the Syrian–Iranian alliance itself.

Chapter 4

After Madrid: local and regional factors

Implications of the peace process for the alliance

Syria's position on the terms of a Middle East settlement has remained constant since Madrid. A number of interesting changes in emphasis have emerged, however, despite the slow pace of the Syrian–Israeli track over the three years of negotiations since 1991. These have included a number of significant Syrian gestures towards Israel and a readiness to speak of 'normal' relations between the two countries after a full settlement. On the other hand, continued Syrian criticism of both Palestinian and Jordanian dealings with Israel since the secret Oslo deal of 1993 and the Israel–Jordan treaty of 1994 reflects a deep concern that the loss of Arab coordination in the negotiations has significantly eroded the prospects for maximizing Arab gains in a settlement and has compromised Syria's own prospects regarding the Golan. Thus, for instance, Syria was highly critical of Jordan's willingness to lease its territory for Israeli use, a precedent that could be prejudicial to Syria's position on Israeli settlements on the Golan. Syria's long-standing distrust of tendencies on the part of the PLO and Jordan to look to their own separate interests has also been reinforced, as have its suspicions of Israeli intentions to divide Arab ranks. But despite its unease regarding the PLO, Syria has held to the view that a truly comprehensive settlement should also be measured by the degree of acceptance of any settlement by the Palestinians themselves. Syria's objections to the Oslo deal have been based in part on the lack of Palestinian consensus regarding it and its divisive and controversial status both inside and outside the Occupied Territories. By way of contrast, a final agreement that was accepted by the majority of Palestinians would satisfy Syrian criteria for equitability and stability and would be non-objectionable (in principle at least) from the Syrian point of view. From a geopolitical perspective Syria still appears to conceive of its relationship with Iran through the prism of 'strategic parity' with Israel, although the concept has not been actively promoted as a central plank of Syrian policy since the beginning of the Madrid process. In its current form 'parity' retains the element of Syrian military strength and deterrent capabilities but is channelled in the interests of Syria's negotiating stance more specifically than before. 'Parity' now requires a sufficient critical mass of Syrian options, relations and means of pressure and persuasion to overcome the imbalance of power with Israel and give a real edge to Syria's negotiating stance. The relationship with Iran is thus seen by Syria as a vital addition to its negotiating strength and its margins of manoeuvre with Israel. In this sense the alliance with Iran has facilitated the negotiations with Israel and the peace process as a whole by reinforcing Syrian self-confidence and lessening its concerns about a straight Israeli diktat based on military power alone. Indeed, one of the more remarkable aspects of the Syrian–Iranian relationship since the Syrian decision to join the peace process has been the relative *decline* in tensions between them. Many of the causes of Syrian–Iranian friction were related to their perceived competition in Lebanon, which reached its height in 1986–7. As this rivalry has receded since the Taif accords of 1989 and as Iran has gradually conceded the primacy of Syrian interests in this arena, other factors, such as Iranian opposition to the peace process, have remained a secondary irritant by comparison. Iran's appreciation of the overall benefits and low costs of maintaining good relations with Syria have thus continued to outweigh the expected returns of rivalry and competition with it in domains that are a vital Syrian concern.

Iran's readiness to coexist with Syria's participation in the peace process has not, however, weakened its own ideological stance towards the peace process. Iran's opposition to an Arab–Israeli settlement has been unwavering and has been expressed increasingly vociferously since the Oslo deal, its objections to which have been on similar lines to those of Syria; but its initial response to the October 1994 Israeli–Jordanian peace treaty was relatively muted, and an Iranian delegation visited Amman shortly after the treaty in order to bolster bilateral relations. Generally, however, Iran's view that the end result of an Arab–Israeli negotiated settlement would be an Israeli–US diktat has not been substantially revised. As it stands today, Iranian policy still brooks no notion of a comprehensive peace with Israel and continues to emphasize its political and ideological opposition to the Jewish state. With no direct territorial or material stake in the process, Iran has adopted a multilayered approach based on attempting to influence Syrian policy on the one hand and on maintaining a foothold in the Palestinian rejectionist camp and the Lebanese arena on the other. Iran's fears of regional isolation in the wake of a settlement also underlie its broader regional strategy of building relations with Islamic movements across the Middle East in anticipation of an escalating campaign by regional parties against 'Iranian-backed extremism'. Alongside the maintenance of its special relationship with the Islamicist regime in Sudan, Iran has sought to improve relations with other key Arab states including Iraq, Egypt and Tunisia as a means of containing the current anti-Iranian tenor of much of Arab policy and increasing its margins of manoeuvre on the Arab scene. This policy appears to have partly paid off, at least in the case of Egypt, which has scaled down its attacks on Iran and backtracked on previous accusations of Iranian involvement with and support for the Egyptian Islamicists.

Iran's relatively restrained official line towards Syrian participation in the peace process reflects its immediate desire not to antagonize its major regional ally at a critical juncture in the area; it also reflects Syria's own presentation of the unfolding negotiating process in bilateral consultations between the two parties. Iranian tolerance of Syrian participation in the talks so far is at least partly based on a Syrian view that stresses the uncertain and tenuous nature of the process itself. Thus although Syria does not deny that it is committed to the process, it stresses its doubts about its ultimate outcome. Syrian suspicions of Israel's intentions and of its readiness to accept a truly comprehensive and equitable settlement remain strong and have been reinforced by constant fluctuations in Israel's emphasis on the Syrian track and its estimation of its political and strategic salience. Syria's readiness to talk to Israel can thus be portrayed as a necessary move based on the imbalance of power but without any illusions as to its end result. Reinforcing Iran's perception of Syrian uncertainty about the negotiations is an underlying Iranian assumption that Syria will not accept a 'sell-out' or an agreement that infringes basic Arab rights. This is not a view universally held in Tehran; it is evident that some of the more radical Iranian tendencies associated with Ayatollah Khamene'i hold a contrary opinion of Syrian policy and the prospects of an Israeli–Syrian agreement, although they remain restrained by the official pro-Syrian line.

Towards a new strategic nexus

The nature of an Arab–Israeli settlement will have a crucial influence on future Syrian–Iranian relations. Open borders, significant trade and commercial relations, and broad political and cultural normalization between Israel and the Arab states generally, and between Syria and Israel more specifically, would clearly entail some adjustment to the current Syrian–Iranian relationship. For the Syrians, however, the achievement of *full* normalization with Israel is unlikely until Israel has completed its withdrawal from the Golan, a process which is likely to be relatively protracted. Syria may therefore seek to keep the pressure up against Israel via its Iranian option, in its various permutations, at least until it is fully confident of Israel's intention to fulfil all its commitments on withdrawal. Syria's interest in its relationship with Iran will thus not be radically affected overnight by the Syrian–Israeli peace process, although longer-term changes may occur as a result of the global effect of Arab–Israeli normalization.

Barring the possibility of a major change in regime or external outlook in either Syria or Iran, both sides' pursuit of their alliance may in fact intensify rather than diminish in the wake of such a settlement. While a comprehensive Arab–Israeli peace should put an end to the prospect of large-scale state-to-state warfare, it will not necessarily obviate all other Arab or Israeli political and security concerns, nor will it automatically erase the deep-seated antagonisms of the past. The transition to a generalized peace and normalized Arab–Israeli relations may be somewhat less than smooth and unproblematic. Much depends on the final terms of a settlement and whether these are generally perceived to be equitable, especially on the Arab/Islamic side. A peace that is seen to reflect Israeli demands and that includes Israel's retention of significant tracts of Arab land may remain unpalatable to many elements within the Arab and Islamic worlds, regardless of the relations between the governments themselves. Furthermore, in its initial phases at least, an Arab–Israeli peace may not be totally undifferentiated. As highlighted by the Israel–Jordan peace treaty and other developments in the process of Arab–Israeli 'normalization', different Arab parties may have different relations with Israel at different times, creating a relatively fluid situation and a possible sense of disorientation and enhanced uncertainty on the part of some of the local and international players. In such conditions new threats and threat perceptions may help to reshape the Syrian–Iranian alliance and create a new set of commonly perceived interests, as well as potential points of friction, between the two parties.

Iran's main concern in the wake of an Arab–Israeli settlement is that a new Arab-Israeli-Western constellation of forces, whether tacit or formal, may develop with Iran itself as its primary designated adversary. This can be seen as one of the main motives behind Iran's current rejectionist stance, although it is reinforced with a politico-ideological overlay. In addition to a Syrian peace accord with Israel, Iran now has to contend with a *de facto* end of Israeli–Iraqi hostilities and possible moves towards a formal Iraqi settlement with Israel, thus relieving Israel of the second of its two remaining major Arab antagonists. Iran's fears of increasing regional isolation should be put in the context of its perceptions of Israeli enmity, of the West's search for a new ideological adversary represented by Iran/'Islamic extremism' and of the continuous struggles between many of the regimes in the area and their own internal Islamic opposition. For the Iranians, therefore, an Arab–Israeli settlement could lead to a situation where Iran is set up as a convenient scapegoat not only for the regional instabilities that will most likely persist after a settlement, but also for other worldwide ills such as transnational 'Islamic terrorism'. Iranian perceptions are that the United States, spurred on by Israel, is casting about for a new rationale for its 'global hegemonistic drive' after the defeat of communism, and has designated Iran as an appropriate successor threat to the Soviet Union.

As an Arab–Israeli settlement will put a final and decisive end to the *military* conflict between Israel and the Arab states, it is indeed possible that international and regional perceptions of the 'Iranian threat' may be heightened and that Iran may be seen as a potential adversary by a number of the parties concerned. There has been no real consensus among the Arab states and Israel so far regarding the salience of the Iranian threat, and most sober views tend to discount the more extreme scenarios regarding Iran's military capabilities and intentions, including its supposed nuclear ambitions, for the short term at least. Much will depend, however, on the degree to which Iran is seen to be actively supporting Islamic and other rejectionist groups within the area and beyond, and thus whether an anti-Iranian coalition of the sort feared by Iran will develop in perceived self-defence against such a threat. A certain amount of self-fulfilling prophecy on both sides may occur here: Iran, out of fear of isolation and aggressive intent on the part of Israel and the West supported by an Arab bloc freed from its fears of Israel, could increase its support for Islamic opposition groups and other radical rejectionist elements in the area; or such an Arab–Israeli-Western coalition could develop as a *pre-emptive* move precisely out of fear of such an activist Iranian policy, fuelling Iran's own response and creating a vicious circle of escalatory action and reaction. In any foreseeable contingency, however, it would appear to be in Iran's vital interest to keep Syria out of any such coalition. Without Syria, major political or military moves against Iran by an Arab bloc allied to Israel and the West would be that much more difficult to realize, although not necessarily impossible (e.g. with Iraq and Jordan, backed by the Gulf states). Syria's good offices and its influence are an important means of reducing the prospects of such a coalition, and it is safe to assume that Tehran has fully absorbed the lessons of Syria's crucial role as a politico-military buffer during the first Gulf war. Conversely, Syrian hostility could be severely detrimental to Iran. As demonstrated by Syrian participation in the coalition against Iraq, Syria could give extra credibility and clout to any future action against a 'pariah' state in the area. Syrian control over Iranian access to Lebanon could also radically affect any future Iranian attempt to utilize Lebanon as a forward base, defensively or offensively. In such circumstances the Iranian interest in actively antagonizing Syria must be minimal.

From both Iran's and Syria's perspectives, an Arab–Israeli settlement is unlikely to affect their mutual interest in maintaining their relationship in the short to medium term. Nevertheless, at the same time developments may take place that could challenge this interest. A substantial reorientation of the Syrian regime after Assad's departure could significantly affect the underlying rationale for the alliance with Iran from the Syrian point of view. A similar shift in Iran's policy is possible under increasing pressure from radical elements newly reinvigorated by the political and economic difficulties facing the Rafsanjani presidency. A newly radicalized Iran may well see a Syrian–Israeli settlement as a political and ideological sell-out. More generally, while it may be premature to speculate in detail about the nature of the new relationships that will develop after a settlement, it is possible that these may diverge sharply from past patterns of alliance and interest. For instance, the emergence of a significant Syrian–Israeli economic or trade relationship could dilute the traditional antagonism between the two countries and hence lessen, *inter alia*, the prospects of an Israeli–Turkish envelopment policy aimed at Syria. This could dissipate those elements of a Syrian–Iranian alliance that may have otherwise emerged in reaction to a perceived Israeli–Turkish axis. A substantial strengthening of Iran's alignment with Iraq, with or without Saddam, would be as likely to strengthen Israel's incentive to improve its relations with Iran as to propel it in the opposite direction. While this in itself neither strengthens nor weakens the possibility of an Israeli–Iranian rapprochement, it is important to note that estimates by senior Israeli security officials regarding the relative weight of the Iraqi and Iranian threats have varied, with the Iraqi threat given occasional precedence.

On the other hand, Israeli relations with Iraq could improve. Recent contacts between the two sides (after an initial flurry in 1986–8) have led to a significant official change in Iraqi policy. Regardless of its short-term response to Iraqi overtures, Israel is likely to view such changes as a means of exerting pressure on both Syria and Iran, especially if Iraq were to declare itself unequivocally in support of an Arab–Israeli settlement and undertake to join a Middle East arms control regime under strict verification conditions and external control. For the Iranians, an opening to Israel could significantly weaken the prospects of any truly effective anti-Iranian coalition emerging in the area without necessarily damaging relations with Syria, given that it would be difficult for the Syrians to object to Iranian–Israeli ties while Syria itself is at peace with Israel.

In short, while the immediate effect of an Arab–Israeli settlement on the regional politico-strategic landscape may be uncertain, it may well lead to a substantial change in many of the established patterns of behaviour and relationships engendered by this conflict over the past decades. Assuming continued movement towards an Israeli–Syrian peace agreement, an eventual shift in the strategic locus in the Mashriq away from the Arab–Israeli conflict is likely to occur. Although Syrian threat perceptions regarding Israel (and vice versa) are unlikely to dissipate overnight, a peace agreement will by definition necessarily curtail the use of force as an element of inter-state relations in the Arab–Israeli arena. In place of the traditional local and international focus on the repercussions of conflict and potential conflagration between Israel and the Arabs (with a specific focus in recent years on Syria), a new strategic nexus may develop centring instead on the triangular relationship between Syria, Turkey and Iran. The emergence of this new strategic nexus will not only affect the three parties themselves but will have an impact on the policy and posture of Iraq, on the situation in the Gulf, and on the regional role of Israel as well as on a host of other related issues.

The Iraqi factor: prospective changes and new alliances

The future of Iraq will continue to be a central politico-strategic concern for both Syria and Iran. The historical rivalry between the Syrian and

Iraqi Baath has been severely exacerbated by Syria's support for the anti-Saddam coalition during the Gulf crisis and war of 1990–1. Assad's decision to join the coalition was crucial in containing Arab criticism of the US-led alliance and in facilitating Western military action against Iraq, while a strong Syrian stance against such action could have severely hampered the coalition's political and operational prospects, given Assad's stature and Syria's regional power and influence. By way of contrast, the Gulf war seems to have lessened Iraqi–Iranian antagonisms, mostly as a result of the reinforcement of Iran's position *vis-à-vis* a significantly weakened Iraq. With no direct threat of Iraqi hegemonism or of renewed military aggression, Iran has been able to afford a relatively sanguine approach to Iraq. For its part, Iraq's interest in reaching out to Iran has been manifest in the conciliatory tone adopted by Saddam in recent public statements and diplomatic dealings with Iran. Since the end of the Gulf war, Saddam has increasingly stressed Iraq's readiness to overcome the legacy of the past and restore the links of Islamic brotherhood in return for Iranian gestures of goodwill such as the return of Iraqi aircraft flown to Iran during the war. Iraq's new stance towards Iran has clearly been dictated by the need to break out of the postwar boycott and the debilitating effects of local and international political and economic isolation. Iran's response to Saddam's overtures has been both cautious and pragmatic. While avoiding active support for Iraq's rehabilitation and reintegration into the international community, Iran has nonetheless called for an early end to UN sanctions and has been willing to assist in the export of Iraqi oil via Iranian territory.

In the emerging new regional environment the long-term survival of Saddam is not necessarily antithetical to Iran's interests. In fact, Iranian relations with Iraq currently appear better on the whole than Syrian–Iraqi relations, despite the legacy of eight years of the Iran–Iraq war. Iran's current policy towards Iraq appears to be based on the following assumptions. First, that the existing Iraqi regime may be more durable than was apparent in the immediate aftermath of the Gulf war and that its eventual rehabilitation may be only a matter of time, given the accumulating local and international pressures in this direction. Second, that a weakened Iraq under Saddam may be preferable to a stronger successor regime freed from the current constraints. One Iranian concern is that such a regime might align itself too closely with the United States, effectively turning into a US 'stooge' or proxy. Equally problematic for Iran would be an eventual Iraqi rapprochement or deal with Israel that could develop over time into an overt or tacit Israeli–Iraqi axis with an active interventionist or protective role in the Gulf against Iran and the fundamentalist threat. Third, that without Saddam, an internally divided Iraq could generate continuous friction and instability on Iran's borders and potentially suck it into conflicts within Iraq itself. Alongside Syria and Turkey, Iran has thus consistently voiced its support for the 'territorial integrity' of Iraq, as well as its concern regarding the establishment of a Western-backed Kurdish enclave in northern Iraq, seen by Iran as 'another Israel'. To the extent that Iraqi Kurdish separatist aspirations encourage similar tendencies among Iran's own Kurdish population, Tehran is not averse to the maintenance of strong central pressure on the Kurds from Baghdad. Equally problematic from an Iranian point of view would be the possibility of direct foreign intervention by Turkey or possibly even Syria itself in Iraq subsequent to a collapse of Saddam or the central authority in Baghdad. With such concerns in mind, Iran may prefer to uphold the status quo as long as this offers the best chance of containing developments in Iraq and the Gulf that could be turned against Iranian interests. At the same time, Iran may wish to maintain the option of manipulating its policy towards Iraq so as to influence Syria and other regional and extra-regional actors. The possibility of a more comprehensive reconciliation with Iraq is thus a potential card to be traded against Syrian concessions and the acknowledgment of Iranian interests elsewhere. This may be especially relevant in Lebanon, given the likelihood that any Israeli-Syrian-Lebanese settlement will require tacit or overt Iranian acceptance of an end to Hizbullah's military operations in South Lebanon.

A number of possible points of tension between Syria and Iran appear at this juncture. A rehabilitated or resurgent Saddam may seek to penalize Syria for its role in both Gulf wars. The precedents of punitive Iraqi support for anti-regime Islamic elements in Syria in 1980–2 and anti-Syrian Maronite elements in Lebanon in 1988–90 have not been forgotten in Damascus. In that sense, the stakes in the long-standing struggle between Assad and Saddam may have been further increased. Unlike Iran, and others such as Turkey, Jordan and Qatar (and potentially even Israel and the West), Syria may find it difficult to adopt a purely 'pragmatic' approach to the current Iraqi regime and may seek to undercut any Iraqi–Iranian rapprochement by strengthening its ties with other Arab parties. In line with its traditional policy Syria will most likely seek to balance any Iraqi–Iranian rapprochement by enhancing its relations with Egypt, as well as by a further cementing of ties with Saudi Arabia, a trend already in evidence in the Egyptian-Syrian-Saudi Alexandria summit of

December 1994. (It is, however, a measure of Syrian concern not to antagonize Iran that a Syrian envoy was dispatched to Tehran to explain the Syrian point of view in the immediate wake of this summit.) Another means of leverage would be a hardening of Syria's position on issues of particular concern to Iran, such as the conflict with the United Arab Emirates over the Abu Musa and Tunb islands in the Gulf.

In dealing with the future of Iraq, including the possibility of an improvement in Iraq–Iran relations, Syrian interests dictate that as much of the Arab Gulf war alliance as possible remains in place. This would partly explain Syria's continued interest in the 1991 Damascus Declaration as a forum for Syrian–Gulf relations. Besides political backing from the Gulf states for its stance on the peace process, Syria has gained other benefits, among them continued financial aid from Saudi Arabia and the other Gulf countries and an increase of its political influence within the Gulf area itself. Syria's prime objective thus appears to be the maintenance of a vital means of pressure against Saddam as well as control over the pace of Gulf 'normalization' with Israel. The Damascus Declaration for the first time affords Syria a direct partnership role in helping to shape current and future Arab policies towards Iraq and other Gulf issues. Syria's Gulf profile has thus been substantially raised since the Gulf war, as was apparent in its active mediation in the Yemeni–Saudi dispute and its role as a channel to Iran during the internal disturbances in Bahrain in early 1995.

Through its continuing alliance with Iran, Syria can contain Iranian initiatives towards Iraq by acting as a counterpoise to Iran's own interest in maintaining good relations with Syria. In the longer term Iran could also be instrumental in supporting Syrian policy objectives towards Iraq, given its influence within the Iraqi Shia community. A friendly Iran could help to block or contain the accession to power of anti-Syrian elements in Iraq after Saddam or in the case of his overthrow. Although Iran has good reason to have an independent policy towards Iraq, it is likely to continue to heed Syrian concerns about such policy (at least in so far as Syria may consider that its own vital interests are at stake), notwithstanding the current stability in Iraq–Iran relations. Excluding the possibility that an Iranian understanding with Iraq would take on an overtly anti-Syrian stance, the Syrian–Iranian relationship appears sufficiently flexible to allow for a relatively wide margin of manoeuvre on either side. Syrian concern about a pro-Iraqi tilt by Iran is mitigated by the close level of political coordination maintained between the two sides, and by the realization that Iran's vital interests in Iraq entail a certain degree of Syrian tolerance and forbearance within mutually acceptable limits.

Regardless of Syrian–Iraqi rivalry, Syria may still view the possibility of a new relationship with Iraq, including a Syria-Iran-Iraq axis, as a viable policy option. Such an option could be appropriate from a Syrian point of view were a serious setback to occur in the current peace process. Despite its strategic commitment to the peace process as a matter of national interest, Syria may seek to maintain its freedom of action should no acceptable settlement be found with Israel, or if other factors should intervene to disrupt the process and throw it into disarray, such as the return of a hardline Likud government in Israel, a collapse in the Israeli–Palestinian interim phase arrangements, internal instability or a succession crisis in Jordan. Syria also needs to take into account the possibility of such a breakdown in a situation where several Arab countries have already achieved an advanced stage of 'normalization' with Israel (Jordan has already signed a final peace treaty with Israel). In such a context, the alliance with Iran could play a crucial role in fortifying Syria's stance and credibility. Iran's value for Syria is further highlighted by the absence of any other Arab party ready or able to play such a role. The regional significance of the Syrian–Iranian alliance would be of a different order altogether were Iraq to join it. Although Iraq may once again risk its prospects of international rehabilitation by alignment with such an overtly 'radical' bloc, it might seriously consider a tripartite axis with Syria and Iran in the continued absence of any real progress towards lifting the sanctions regime in the short to medium term (particularly after its recognition of Kuwait and overtures towards Israel). An alliance with Syria and Iran could also provide it with an irresistible opportunity to reassert its role as a major regional player. For its part, Iran may be interested in bolstering its regional presence and security through the formation of a powerful new rejectionist bloc that would circumscribe Israel's strategic dominance and the US sphere of influence in the area as well as help undermine the US policy of dual containment. Even without a complete breakdown in the peace talks Syrian, Iraqi and Iranian interests might coincide. Assuming long-drawn-out and inconclusive negotiations stretching beyond the limits of Syrian expectations and tolerance, Syria may consider a reconciliation with the Iraqi regime as a means of radically reshaping the existing regional geostrategic balance in the face of perceived Israeli obduracy. At the very least, Syria may want such a 'worst-case' possibility to be taken seriously by both the United States and Israel. The various Syria-Iran-Iraq scenarios may thus be seen in Damascus as a means of bolstering Syria's negotiating posture and providing it with additional pressure points against Israel and other parties in the area such as Turkey.

A Syria-Iran-Iraq grouping could also be a possible option for Syria in the case of a serious post-settlement rift with Israel. In this instance, Syria may consider the formation of such a bloc not necessarily as an alternative to the peace process, but rather as a means of consolidating its regional position *after* a settlement in anticipation of the emergence of other new political or economic blocs in the area. One particularly pressing Syrian concern is that Israel might emerge as the dominant political and economic force in the Mashriq, drawing Jordan–Palestine and potentially even Iraq within its direct orbit and acting with free and open access to Gulf finance and markets. The combination of Syria, Iraq and Iran would clearly provide further leverage for all three parties against Israel and its potential satellites, and any other regional bloc or grouping. A tripartite axis of this nature after an Arab–Israeli settlement (particularly post-Saddam) would also be in a powerful bargaining position *vis-à-vis* the West, Turkey and the Gulf states.

The exacerbation of Syrian–Iraqi antipathy in the wake of the second Gulf war does not totally preclude the possibility of a self-interested re-establishment of some workable relationship between the two sides, even without a change of regime or leadership in Iraq. At one level, the root cause of this antipathy lies in the historical rivalry between their respective political leaderships, not in any significant or unmanageable set of disputes over territory or resources. Both Assad and Saddam have found common ground in the past when their vital interests so dictated, as in the admittedly short-lived plans for Iraqi–Syrian unification in the aftermath of the Camp David accords in 1978 and the subsequent attempt at reconciliation in early 1987 at the height of the Iran–Iraq war. Iraq also acted unilaterally in support of Syria during the 1973 war, despatching a major military contingent to the Golan front even without prior operational cooperation or the prelude of a political detente with Damascus. The estrangement between the two sides has not been total or complete. The Iraqi minister for water resources joined his Syrian counterpart in discussions over trilateral water issues with Turkey in early 1994, and other low-level political and diplomatic contacts including cultural exchanges and visits have been maintained over the years, despite their limited impact on the overall relationship. In effect, a political decision by both sides to upgrade their relations in face of some common concern or threat cannot be completely discounted. One possibility is that recent

Iraqi overtures to Israel may provide the incentive for a Syrian move to improve relations with Baghdad. Although Assad may not be willing to jeopardize his relations with the United States and the Gulf states in the current political climate, he may also be concerned that an Israeli–Iraqi deal could be used to outflank Syria and increase pressure on it to accede to Israeli demands in the peace talks. The dangers of an Israeli–Iraqi deal would be magnified from a Syrian point of view were it to include Jordan as an active third partner, in the light of the Israeli–Jordanian peace treaty and the traditionally close links between King Hussein and the Iraqi regime. Iraqi–Israeli overtures may thus help to cement Syrian–Iranian ties, at least in the near term. It is most likely, however, that Syria will continue to count on US and Gulf pressure on Israel to abort any opening to Saddam in the immediate future. But Israel's interest in removing Iraq from the circle of confrontation – and perhaps looking towards a post-settlement Tel Aviv-Baghdad-Amman axis – has to be taken seriously in Damascus and it may be difficult to defer some sort of Israeli–Iraqi deal indefinitely. A change of regime in Iraq, however, would undoubtedly help to create a new environment for Syria and Iraq alike, as would a possible shift in Syrian policy post-Assad. But other things being constant, any Syrian–Iraqi detente is likely to be limited in scope and effect as long as the current leadership in both countries remains in power.

In most foreseeable circumstances, Iran is likely to accept any relative improvement in bilateral Syrian–Iraqi ties in much the same manner as Syria appears to be regarding the current Iraqi–Iranian rapprochement. But in the longer term, and as Iraq emerges from its current isolation, Iraqi power and self-assertiveness may pose a new set of dilemmas for the alliance. A more stable and active Syrian–Iraqi bloc could be problematic from the Iranian point of view and could jeopardize the Syrian–Iranian relationship itself. A resurgent Iraq with Western and Gulf support could play the role of senior partner in a new common Arab approach to Iran. Led by the powerful combination of Syria and Iraq, such an approach could threaten Iran's dominance of the Gulf and would suggest the formation of a new Arab Western front directed against Iran. Conversely, an Iraqi alignment with Israel or Jordan (or both) would add to Iran's incentive to maintain the alliance with Syria. Iranian fears from an Israeli presence in the Gulf would be doubly reinforced by Iraq's facilitation of such a presence or its active collusion with it. In such circumstances the Syrian counterbalance would appear crucial from the Iranian point of view.

The Lebanese factor: Syria's interests come first

Syria's vital geopolitical and strategic concerns in Lebanon will not be diminished by any peace agreement with Israel. On the contrary, one of the short- to medium-term consequences of such an agreement is an increased Syrian interest in maintaining a firm grip on relations with Lebanon and in binding it even closer to Syria, as has been evident in the recent series of cooperative agreements and understandings between the two countries. Much of the groundwork for such a close relationship was already laid by the 1989 Taif accords, but Syria's concern to keep Lebanon within its direct orbit is likely to be heightened in the wake of a settlement by an Israel-Palestine-Jordan economic grouping or any similar association comprising other major regional powers, such as a pro-Western constellation comprising Egypt, Israel, Turkey and Saudi Arabia. Lebanon will therefore continue to be viewed as a combination of strategic buffer, politico-economic partner and vital zone of influence for Syria. It is thus likely that Syria will want to consolidate its power base in Lebanon by maintaining its alliance with Iran, especially in view of the importance of the Lebanese Shia community and the likelihood of Iran's continuing influence within it. Given the uncertainties of the post-settlement era, Syria will most probably seek to avoid the creation of new and dangerous challenges for itself by either an unnecessary confrontation with Lebanese pro-Iranian groups or the severance of its ties with Iran in a manner that would seriously jeopardize its interests in Lebanon.

The importance of Lebanon for Iran reaches beyond its spiritual and political ties with the Lebanese Shia. Without access to Lebanon, Iran would be largely severed from the Mashriq at large. Iran thus needs Lebanon to maintain its influence within this arena, whether as spoiler or as facilitator, and will not give up whatever advantages accrue to it from such influence without substantial trade-offs elsewhere. The Iranian presence in Lebanon will also affect and be affected by developments within the broader Islamic fundamentalist movement in the area. From this perspective, Syria is likely to view its relationship with Iran as a means by which it can continue to observe, influence and maintain a measure of control over the Islamic movement in Lebanon and its Arab extensions at relatively minimal cost and effort. An overt and quantifiable Iranian-Islamic presence in Lebanon is also preferable to a covert and unquantifiable presence in Syria itself, especially given the history of conflict between the regime and Islamic activist, albeit Sunni, movements. It may also be in Syria's interest to continue to tolerate the presence of semi-autonomous Iranian proxies in Lebanon as potential pressure points against other local or extra-regional powers, and as a broad concession to Iranian interests in the Arab east as long as nothing is done by such groups to compromise Syria's own concerns. Much the same considerations would apply to any other radical secular groups that may continue to be aligned with Iran after an Arab–Israeli peace settlement and that may maintain a presence or be based in Lebanon.

Syria's tolerance of a certain level of Iranian involvement in Lebanon will depend in part on what transformation occurs among the pro-Iranians there (especially Hizbullah) and whether such groups are willing to adapt to Syria's post-settlement interests, primarily the absolute cessation of military operations against Israel from Lebanese soil. Among the more important of current developments in the Lebanese political scene has been the emergence of a more 'Lebanonized' trend among the traditionally pro-Iranian constituency within the Shia community. Represented to a large extent by Sheikh Hussein Fadlallah (who holds no official position in Hizbullah but is generally regarded as its spiritual leader), this trend has sought to distance itself from Iran's material levers of power as well as its ideological tutelage. Fadlallah and other influential elements within the leadership of Hizbullah have long been aware that the national consensus in support of its armed struggle against Israel's occupation of South Lebanon (a consensus that also strongly reflects Syria's own influence and attitude) does not extend to its other long-term ideological commitments, including the continued rejection of peace and coexistence with Israel, and the promotion of an Islamic government in Lebanon. The major trend within Hizbullah is thus cognizant of the need to conform to the realities of a possible settlement between Israel and both Syria and Lebanon, and of the limitations of attempting to extend an Islamic-style government to the most sectarian and religiously diverse country in the area. This has been reflected in the readiness of Hizbullah to participate in the Lebanese political system, as evidenced by the relatively strong showing of pro-Hizbullah candidates in the 1992 parliamentary elections. As well as demonstrating the party's willingness to abide by the rules of the regenerated Lebanese political system and to relegate its covert activities to a domain that is not directed against the state as such, Hizbullah's current stance places less stress on achieving Islamic government in Lebanon and more on its right to the assertion of Islamic values from within the system itself.

A settlement between Israel and both Syria and Lebanon will confront

Hizbullah with some difficult choices. Much of Hizbullah's appeal and influence has been based on the general resonance of its ideological stance on the Arab–Israeli conflict and its sustained resistance to Israel's occupation of Lebanese soil for over a decade. Hizbullah's acts of resistance have thus become integral to its mystique and *raison d'être* and constitute the most outstanding distinction between it and other parties in Lebanon, including competing forces within the Shia community itself such as Amal. An eventual withdrawal of Israel from South Lebanon will be portrayed as a vindication of Hizbullah's activist line and may serve to provide it with some political capital during the initial post-settlement period in its attempt to maintain and build upon its popular base. Hizbullah is careful to confine its attacks to occupied Lebanese territory, except when provoked into retaliation across the border, and has strongly intimated that an Israeli withdrawal from South Lebanon will end its armed activities against Israel. As is recognized by Hizbullah itself, the post-settlement security regime – to be agreed and insisted upon by Israel, Syria and Lebanon alike – will almost certainly preclude a credible military option in any case. Hizbullah will also have to contend with a general mood among the Shia and across the Lebanese politico-sectarian landscape that will put redevelopment and reconstruction as the overriding Lebanese priorities, a mood that already permeates the Lebanese political system and can only be enhanced by the onset of peace. This feeling is also likely to be particularly strong in South Lebanon itself, traditionally one of the most neglected and needy of Lebanon's regions. Hizbullah has already succeeded in establishing a reservoir of goodwill within its own community in the south and elsewhere (such as the Bikaa and the southern suburbs of Beirut) precisely by helping to provide social and welfare services where none have existed. It will thus be reluctant to antagonize its grassroots support by bringing about renewed conflict and confrontation with Israel or the Lebanese and Syrian authorities that could jeopardize the prospects of a better future for the very constituency it has represented and catered for so far.

In the wake of a settlement Hizbullah may also have to look harder at possible political competition from Amal. Although both Shia parties – after some initial intense friction – have succeeded in establishing a working relationship with some division of roles between them, Amal's political threat to Hizbullah may intensify if the latter opts out of the system or chooses a direct confrontation with it. Given the importance of political patronage in the Lebanese system, Amal's long-standing links with Syria and the Lebanese political establishment and its good relations with the active and prosperous Shia business community at home and aboad may stand it in good stead in any future political or electoral showdown with a radical movement that has lost its function as a means of military pressure against Israel. For this reason and others, the current trend in Hizbullah towards redefining its political Islamic platform seems more than likely to be sustained. Since the acceleration of the peace process, both Islamic and Arab nationalist circles have repeatedly voiced their concern about possible Israeli economic domination as well as Western/Israeli cultural penetration of the Arab and Islamic world in the wake of a settlement. Hizbullah and other Islamic movements in the area hope to benefit from such concerns within Lebanon and elsewhere, with a programme that stresses the need to confront 'cultural and economic normalization' with Israel rather than a singular platform of armed struggle. The Islamic-Arab Nationalist convocation held in Lebanon in October 1994 and attended by a large number of Lebanese and other Islamic and nationalist figures, including Fadlallah, may be the harbinger of such a movement. This sort of approach would emulate to a large extent the policy pursued by the Islamicists in Jordan, where the movement has sought to constrain the freedom of action of the regime in developing ties with Israel rather than seeking an all-out confrontation with it over the issue of a settlement. Consistent with its doctrinal precepts, Hizbullah may seek to make common cause with the Arab nationalist and rejectionist elements inside and outside Lebanon who share its concerns and who may look to it as a natural focus for oppositional activity to the peace process.

A transition of this nature in Hizbullah's policy and posture will not occur overnight. Much depends on the balance of opinion within the movement and the ultimate position taken by Iran, as well as on Hizbullah's overall relationship with Syria. The official leadership of Hizbullah, including its current Secretary General, Sheikh Hassan Nasrallah, enjoys good relations with both Syria and Iran and is as likely to be responsive to the requirements and sensitivities of the former as it is to the latter. The emergence of a growing rift between elements supportive of Fadlallah's independent line and others closer to the pro-Iranian line has been evident for some time and may develop into a more serious organizational split. Iran's final position is also unclear given the competing centres of power dealing with Hizbullah in Tehran and the apparent lack of any centralized control over these links. A radical Hizbullah splinter-group aided and abetted by equally radical (i.e. anti-Rafsanjani) elements in Tehran could decide to pursue its own independent and actively militant line against Israel. This could be bolstered by Palestinian rejectionist groups acting under a similiar Iranian aegis. So far, however, Tehran has not indicated by word or deed that its ideological opposition to the peace process binds it to a commitment to abort this process by military means. For both Iran and Hizbullah in all its tendencies, as well as the major part of Lebanese, Arab and Islamic opinion, the movement's resistance activities in South Lebanon will remain legitimate until agreement is reached on a full and final Israeli withdrawal. Any attempt to undermine such an agreement after its finalization will have considerably less legitimacy and will to that extent marginalize any group that espouses it.

From the Iranian point of view the cost of supporting such a revisionist policy may be too high. Syria's dominance in Lebanon and its ability to block any significant Iranian moves in this arena are such that a direct challenge to Syrian vital interests by Hizbullah or Iran is unlikely to end in any positive Iranian gain. Indeed, the potential loss of access to the Lebanese Shia could be a major deterrent to any Iranian spoiler role as well as a major incentive for Iran to encourage Hizbullah to abide by the new post-settlement rules of the game. A *modus vivendi* between Iran and pro-Iranian forces in Lebanon and Syria under such conditions may be attainable. In return, Syria may be willing to allow Iran and its local allies a certain margin of social and political freedom of action within Lebanon and among the Shia community in particular, including continued Iranian support for health, education and social welfare institutions in this arena.

Syria's interest in preserving its ties with the Lebanese Shia as a potential power base, and Iran's interest in maintaining its access to the largest and most strategically placed Shiite community in the Mashriq, may thus continue to converge over the medium to long term. However, assuming a certain degree of internal political and economic stability in Lebanon, the Lebanese Shia themselves may seek progressively to disengage from the close association with Damascus that has marked Shia politics since the late 1960s. Shia self-confidence and self-assertion may well erode the perceived need for Syrian patronage, especially if the Shiite share of internal power and influence were to develop in a post-settlement Lebanon. In this context, the Shia may seek to develop their relations with Iran as a means of leverage against Syria and in order to contain Syrian influence in Lebanon. Conversely, the Shiite connection to Iran may appear of diminishing import in the wake of a Syrian–Lebanese settlement with Israel. As the military struggle with Israel loses its relevance and rationale, and assuming a gradual and relative revival of the Lebanese polity and economy, the Iranian role that emerged out of the local and regional environment of the early 1980s may begin to wane. Either way, the Lebanese Shia community is bound to be affected by internal developments within Iran itself. The continuing deterioration of the Iranian economy, as well as persistent internal power struggles in Tehran, could impinge upon Iran's material ability to act in Lebanon as well as its moral standing as a role model for Hizbullah and the Shia community at large. Nonetheless, bearing in mind the intimate relationship between the Shiite leadership in the two countries, as well as Iran's traditional influence among the Lebanese Shia even before the revolution, it is unlikely that Iran will lose its Lebanese foothold altogether as a result of such developments.

The Turkish factor: common ground and points of tension

A resolution of the conflict with Israel will not necessarily mitigate Syria's sense of threat or potential threat from other regional actors. Indeed, the dominance of the conflict with Israel since 1948 may have helped to disguise and suppress other latent problems on Syria's northern flank that could now come to the fore. Syrian–Turkish relations may thus face a new period of strain with tensions arising from any or all of the following factors:

- the dispute over Syria's perceived support for the Kurds;
- the dispute over Euphrates water rights;
- regional competition, resulting from a more active Turkish regional posture;
- possible differences over the future of Iraq;
- possible concerns resulting from regional political or military axes or realignments that include Turkey but exclude Syria;
- a resurgence of historic/territorial disputes such as that over Iskandaroun.

Despite recent friction over Armenia and Azerbaijan, and continuing Turkish suspicions regarding Iranian links with Turkish Islamic extremists, Iranian–Turkish relations have been relatively stable over the past few years. Nonetheless, new challenges to this relationship may emerge out of an Arab–Israeli settlement as a result of any or all of the following developments:

- more active Israeli–Turkish or Arab–Turkish cooperation against Iran and/or Iranian-backed movements in the area;
- a more assertive Turkish regional profile, including a stronger interventionist policy in Iraq and/or against the Kurds;
- a new Turkish military or economic role in the Gulf, limiting Iran's perceived regional role and influence;
- 'anti-Iranian' regional alliances that include Arab parties and/or Israel alongside Turkey;
- Turkish brokerage of greater Israeli access to the newly independent republics of former Soviet Central Asia and Azerbaijan.

Both Syria and Iran can thus be seen to have an interest in a continuing alliance that serves to contain Turkey. For Syria, Iran is a countervailing weight against Turkey or any other possible regional reconfiguration of forces including Turkey that may develop out of a comprehensive Arab–Israeli settlement. Likewise, Iran may seek to curb perceived Turkish regional and Central Asian activism (whether by Turkey alone or in conjunction with Israel and the West) through the retention of Syria as a counterweight and as a possible means of pressure on Turkey's southern flank. In the immediate context of Israeli–Syrian negotiations, the Turkish factor could also have an impact on the bilateral Israeli–Syrian security regime, with Syria resisting Israeli demands for deep cuts or radical restructuring of its armed forces on the grounds that this would have an adverse effect on Syria's balance of power with Turkey. Similar problems could also arise within the multilateral negotiations over a new regional arms control regime should Syria join the talks or should these talks be eventually extended to include Iran.

On a broader range of issues Syrian–Turkish and Iranian–Turkish tensions could further be reflected in the development and possible strengthening of Israeli–Turkish ties. Turkish overtures to Israel have stressed the common threats to and interests of the two countries and have been translated practically into projects for joint exploitation of water resources, defence production and other joint economic ventures in Central Asia and China, as well as intelligence cooperation against 'Islamic extremists' across the region. Such developments in Israeli–Turkish relations are of some concern to Syria. Iranian concerns as to the negative consequences of an Arab–Israeli settlement may also be heightened should Turkey appear ready to take a leading anti-Iranian role in concert with overtly hostile powers such as Israel. Any Turkish support for Israeli economic penetration or military aid and covert action in

Azerbaijan and other parts of central Asia is equally likely to arouse Iranian concerns.

A Turkish rapprochement with Iraq could also raise tension with Syria and Iran. Current Turkish policies continue to stress the national interest in economic normalization with Saddam's regime and the need for a lifting of sanctions once Saddam abides by the relevant UN Resolutions. Improved Turkish–Iraqi relations could confront Syria with the prospect of a strategic encirclement if matched with a significant improvement in Turkish ties with Israel and/or close relations between Israel and Jordan. Iran's desire to keep its own options open in respect of Iraq as a potential means of leverage in its relations with the Arabs and the West could also be undermined by Turkish moves towards the Iraqi regime.

However, the degree of current or latent tension between Turkey and either Iran or Syria should not be overstated. Syria's overriding interest in ensuring its access to water resources under Turkish control acts as a deterrent to any significant Syrian escalation against Turkey. Its indirect patronage of Kurdish insurgents such as the PKK can be seen as an instance of Syria's long-standing use of proxies against its potential antagonists, often essentially as a means of exerting pressure to be finally exchanged as part of a political deal on terms acceptable to Syria. In this sense, Syrian support for Turkish Kurdish insurgents represents a potential card to be played in the dispute over water rights or any other current or future point of contention with Turkey. Syria's concern to avoid flagrant provocation of Turkey has already been reflected in the bilateral agreement on a security protocol in April 1994, committing Syria to the prevention of activity hostile to Turkey from Syrian soil, and the steps it has taken to reduce the PKK's presence in Lebanon (such as shutting down its training camps in the Bikaa). Iran has similarly shown extreme caution in dealing with the conflict between Azerbaijan and Armenia and has been wary of any direct confrontation with Turkey that could exacerbate Iran's problems on its northern flank, in Iraq or with the Kurds. For its part, Turkey appears aware that there are limits to its power to restrain either Syria or Iran. Despite some threats of direct action against purported PKK bases in Lebanon, Turkey's ability to undertake such a mission effectively is severely curtailed by both operational considerations and the political repercussions that would follow. All three parties appear to be sufficiently aware of the dangers of any overt conflict between them to have formed joint economic and security committees and to maintain regular contacts over Iraqi and Kurdish-related issues since the Gulf war. Equally, the three seem to have settled on a policy towards Iraq that precludes the break-up of that country (and thus possible Kurdish or Shiite 'independence' in Iraq), although this may disguise significant differences between them on these and other issues.

Syria and Iran have maintained a high degree of interest in and coordination with Turkey in the trilateral ministerial coordination committee set up since 1991 to monitor developments in Iraq and formulate a common approach to Iraq's future. The three parties' concern about border instability, particularly Kurdish in-fighting or a resumption of full-scale Kurdish–Iraqi hostilities, has been sufficient to prevent the sometimes substantial differences between them from spilling over into any sharp open split over the Iraqi question. But the actual response of any of the three to a major Iraqi crisis remains uncertain. Both Syria and Iran are likely to view with grave concern any large-scale Turkish military intervention in northern Iraq and there has already been some Iranian–Turkish tension as a result of Turkish incursions against the PKK in northern Iraq that have spilled over into Iranian territory proper. Syrian and Iranian reactions to more substantial intervention will be largely determined by their perceptions of the situation within Iraq and Turkey's underlying political and strategic objectives. Both are more likely to react negatively if they see Turkey as aiming for a permanent or long-term military presence on Iraqi soil or if its objectives appear to go beyond certain acceptable limits such as containment of the Kurds. By the same token, an Iranian military move in support of a Shiite secessionist movement, or one that aims to pre-empt other third-party external intervention in Iraq, could push Syria towards a closer relationship with Turkey and severely strain Iran's relations with Syria. The experience of the recent past, however, and its proven caution and reticence during the post-Gulf war Shia uprising, suggest that Iran is unlikely to make such a move. In the absence of such major developments, the trilateral committee and other diplomatic contacts provide an important means of crisis management and serve to lock all three parties into a mutually beneficial bond that limits the ability of any one side to exploit potential Iraqi contingencies at the expense of the other two. The committee and other continuing consultations can thus be seen as a useful mechanism for stabilizing the relationship of the three parties within the boundaries of their common interests in Iraq.

Nonetheless, until the contours of the post-Arab–Israeli settlement era emerge more clearly, the prospect of a regionally active Turkey aided by the West and in tacit or open alliance with Israel and/or Iraq will continue to give both Syria and Iran a strong incentive to look towards each other.

Syria may hope to build on existing Turkish–Iranian tensions and rivalries, although it is unlikely that it would want to be drawn into any direct role in Central Asia (e.g. in Armenia and Azerbaijan). Iran may similarly hope to build upon Syrian concerns about Turkey without being drawn into Syrian–Turkish tensions over the Euphrates waters. Given Turkey's demographic weight and its military and economic power, and even in the best of circumstances where bilateral relations between Syria and Turkey and Turkey and Iran are relatively friction-free, a Syrian–Iranian axis is still likely to be seen in Damascus and Tehran as instrumental in curbing Turkish regional ambitions and in preventing a decisive shift in the regional balance of power against both parties.

The Gulf factor: managing separate interests

In the event of an Arab–Israeli settlement Syria's traditional role as intermediary between the Gulf states and Iran may assume additional value to both Iran and these states, given possible Iranian feelings of insecurity and isolation after such a settlement. While the Gulf war initially appeared to re-establish some degree of mutual confidence in Iranian–Gulf relations, other sources of tension between the two sides have arisen that could be increasingly problematic. These include Syria's support for Abu Dhabi in the escalating verbal conflict over Iran's annexation of Abu Musa, as confirmed at the January 1995 Damascus Declaration meeting in Cairo, Iran's continuing military, political and ideological competition with Saudi Arabia, and its readiness to deal with Iraq. In this context, both the Gulf states and the West may attach continuing value to Syria's ability to approach Iran over Gulf-related issues. In early 1992 Syria's mediatory role on the Abu Musa dispute was given much prominence in the wake of a visit to Tehran by the Syrian Vice-President, Abdul-Halim Khaddam. The internal Shiite disturbances in Bahrain in early 1995 were also the occasion of a Syrian effort to mediate between Tehran and Manama. It is important, however, to note the limitations of Syria's Iranian connection in this respect. Syria has not credibly demonstrated any great moderating influence on Iran's Gulf policies over the past few years, and Iran has equally shown itself to be adept at exploiting inter-Gulf differences to its advantage. At the same time, a number of Gulf states, including Qatar, Oman and Kuwait, have maintained correct and largely cordial relations with Iran, especially since the end of the Iran–Iraq war, thus allowing for direct Iranian–Gulf contacts that may lessen the need for a separate Syrian connection.

Syria will nevertheless continue to be seen as an important element in crisis management with Iran, even if not necessarily as the only channel to Tehran or even the best one under all foreseeable circumstances. From a Gulf point of view, the Syrian–Iranian axis remains a critical restraint on Saddam, as well as a potential constraint on Iran's own freedom of action in the Gulf, in Iraq or elsewhere. For its part Syria will continue to see its Iranian connection as a useful tool in its dealings with the Gulf. Given that the politico-strategic environment in the Gulf is determined more by the nature of Saudi–Iranian relations than any other bilateral set of local relationships, Syria will remain well placed to harness this situation in favour of its own political and economic interests with both parties, and will seek to avoid having to choose between its close ties with either country or display any clear bias in any Saudi–Iranian bilateral dispute.

The fact that the Damascus Declaration grouping formally abandoned any aspirations towards a collective security function by 1992 may be advantageous to Syria in its dealings with Iran. The maintenance of this grouping gives weight and credibility to any Syrian Gulf role, but its non-military character helps to reassure the Iranians as to the limits of this role. At the same time, Syria's initial interest in a Gulf security role suggests that it was willing – in principle at least – to partake in a function and structure that met with Iran's disapproval, thus once again affirming the primacy of Syrian national interests over the Iranian connection. A change of heart within the GCC regarding an expanded Arab security role in the Gulf may rekindle Syrian interest and pose a new problem for the alliance with Iran, although much would depend on the nature and circumstances of such a move.

A major Iranian concern after an Arab–Israeli settlement will be the effect this may have on the balance of power in the Gulf. One Iranian threat perception centres on the possibility that the West's presence in the Gulf could be further reinforced by an Israeli role in the area, including new trade and economic relations and potentially even an indirect military role through arm sales and logistical support activities. From an Iranian perspective, a Syrian presence in the Gulf is a preferable substitute to and constraint upon any Israeli deep penetration of the area or a continued and progressively more aggressively oriented Western presence, although it is unclear as to what Syria's margins of manoeuvre might be in this respect. Nonetheless, such Iranian concerns, as well as Syria's own likely interest in limiting the extent of Israel's presence in the Gulf, could help to develop a common Syrian–Iranian approach to this issue. It would be difficult for the GCC countries to ignore such a joint approach, especially if Syria and Iran were both still perceived to be essential elements in the containment of Iraq.

Syrian–Iranian interests in the Gulf also extend to the potential course of Gulf–Iraqi relations. As long as the general consensus against Saddam Hussein holds, Syrian and Iranian relations with the other Gulf countries are likely to remain largely stable, and bilateral relations between Syria and Iran are unlikely to be severely strained by developments within the Gulf, barring any major crises or open conflict between Iran and Saudi Arabia. However, new problems could arise if there were to be a change of regime in Iraq or if the existing regional consensus against Saddam were to fall apart. A new Iraqi regime closely aligned with Iran could pose a potential threat to Syrian–Iranian relations if Syria were excluded, both directly and inasmuch as it could also be seen as a threat to the Gulf and Syria's Gulf interests. A full-scale Iranian rapprochement with Saddam could also undermine Syrian–Iranian relations and have a negative impact on Syria's Gulf role by undercutting Syria's supposed ability to influence Iran to the Gulf's advantage. By contrast, Gulf fears of any such developments, including the threat of a Syria-Iran-Iraq axis, will continue to strengthen both Syria's and Iran's hands in the Gulf and in inter-Arab affairs generally.

The Palestinian factor: diminishing returns for the rejectionists

The Palestinian factor has not been a particular bone of contention between Syria and Iran in recent years. Both countries have been deeply critical of the PLO's alignment with Iraq during the Iran–Iraq war, its perceived ideological sell-out of Palestinian national aspirations, and its separate political and diplomatic dealings with Israel culminating in the September 1993 accord. The deterioration of PLO–Iranian relations can be traced back to a number of significant differences between the two sides that came to the fore soon after the revolution. One major factor was the ideological tension between the PLO's national secular outlook and the Iranian view of Islam as the necessary bedrock for any authentic revolutionary struggle in the area. As early as Arafat's first (and only) visit to Iran in February 1979, Iranian leaders (including Ayatollah Montazeri and Hashemi Rafsanjani) urged upon the Palestinians the need to adopt Islam and *Jihad* as the principal basis for action. Although the Iranian leadership subsequently reconciled itself to dealing with other secular (including Marxist 'atheist') Palestinian opposition groups,

Iran's loss of faith in the PLO's ideological outlook and its insistence on its broad-based national character appear to have eroded the previous Iranian belief in the 'purity' and sanctity of the Palestinian movement. The Palestinian readiness to strike a deal was another blow to Iran's somewhat inflated expectations of the PLO. A PLO attempt to mediate with Iran over the fate of the US hostages held in the American embassy in 1980 was thus ill received and considered unbefittting to a revolutionary movement. For the Iranians, the PLO was merely trying to extract some selfish gain out of a crisis faced by a sister movement. When the then Palestinan ambassador in Tehran, Hani al-Hassan, publicly tried to claim credit for the release of a number of black hostages held at the embassy, Khomeini's own office issued a strongly worded denial. Further differences arose from PLO contacts with anti-Khomeini groups such as Massoud Rajawi's Mujahidin, and the PLO's refusal to condemn the Soviet invasion of Afghanistan (which aborted an active Palestinian attempt to mediate between the Iranians and the USSR), but most significantly over the Iran–Iraq war.

At first, Iran attempted to use the PLO's good offices to try to contain Arab support for Iraq, and to keep Iranian channels open to the Gulf states. At a time when the Syrian–Iranian relationship had not yet blossomed into a full-scale alliance, such a PLO role made sense from the Iranian point of view. Arafat's initial posture against 'the acquisition of territory by force' also gave some credence to the Iranian belief that the PLO would stand behind Iran as a matter of principle. In December 1980, a high-level Iranian delegation headed by Hashemi Rafsanjani, then head of the *Shwara* (Consultative) Assembly, met with Arafat and the Palestinian leadership in Beirut to urge upon it a more active pro-Iranian role among the Arabs. But this and subsequent consultations only appeared to deepen the Iranian sense of disillusionment with the PLO. From the Palestinian point of view, the Iranians seemed unwilling or unable to understand the PLO's delicate position in the inter-Arab balance and the limitations this imposed on its ability to influence Arab parties already fearful of Iran's revolutionary message and potential impact. By 1981, the Iranians had lost hope in the PLO as an ally and had begun to seek a regional substitute via the alliance with Syria. Given Syria's own longstanding tensions with the PLO and the emerging Iranian belief that state-to-state relations with Syria were a significantly more effective means of affecting the regional environment, by 1982 and the Israeli invasion of Lebanon the PLO–Iranian relationship had become largely relegated to the status of bitter nostalgia on both sides.

For these and other reasons, such as local rivalries in Lebanon, both Syria and Iran have given considerable political and material backing to anti-Arafat Palestinian opposition groups, particularly since 1991, and have tended to lend the same bloc of Palestinian Islamic and secular rejectionists varying degrees of support. Syrian–Palestinian relations are, however, to be differentiated from those between Iran and the Palestinians. Unlike Iran, which has renounced its support for the PLO (but still recognizes the Palestinian 'state' embassy in Tehran), Syria has not broken off relations with the organization. It has nonetheless established little or no contact with the Gaza/Jericho-based Palestine National Authority (PNA) or its leadership, including Arafat himself, since late 1993. At the same time, Syrian ties with Palestinian opposition groups appear undiminished and contacts with PLO figures known to be critical of Arafat and the Oslo deal have been maintained. Besides preserving its own interests within the Palestinian camp, Syria has also facilitated Iranian ties with these groups, both in its tutelary role in its Lebanese domain and in its traditional capacity as a politico-operational base and relatively safe haven for Palestinian rejectionism. Syrian facilitation of Iranian contacts with the Palestinian opposition helps to set a ceiling on Palestinian rejectionism and keep it within the bounds of what Syria knows and considers relatively tolerable. Since 1991 Syrian and Iranian efforts have centred on the 'Group of Ten' Palestinian organizations and splinter groups including Hamas, Shikaki's Islamic Jihad, Habash's PFLP, Hawatmeh's PDF, Jibril's PFLP-GC, Abu Musa's Fateh, the *intifada* and the Syrian-backed Saiqa. Despite Syrian and Iranian encouragement, however, the 'Group of Ten' has failed to develop a common political programme due to sharp differences over the relative weight of the parties concerned and important political and ideological differences between them. Most of its constituents have consequently developed their own separate channels to the various power centres in Damascus and Tehran and have established their own networks with both parties to the alliance.

The Palestinian rejectionist groups have been seen in Damascus and Tehran as an important means of influencing the internal Palestinian balance and as a potential instrument of state policy towards other actors, primarily Israel and the United States, affording the possibility of taking certain positions and indirect actions while maintaining political distance and deniability. For both Damascus and Tehran this reflects more than an apparent tendency to manipulate Palestinian elements to fit their own respective purposes; it is equally a reflection of their political and ideological sympathy with the parties concerned. Syria has been a champion of the Palestinian right to armed struggle since the very beginning of Fateh armed activity in the early 1960s; and, notwithstanding its recent estrangement from the PLO, Iran's revolutionary tradition and its historically intimate relations with the Palestinian movement have left a strong legacy of empathy and support for the Palestinian underdog in the struggle against Israel. At the same time, the Palestinian groups concerned have generally been willing to tolerate whatever constraints arise from external Syrian–Iranian patronage in return for a certain level of political presence and visibility. For some of the smaller splinter groups, their very viability might be questionable but for such patronage, and external support may have been crucial in ensuring their continued existence over the past years. For the major groups such as the PFLP, PDF and Hamas, the relationship is more complex. Not only are such groups deeply rooted in the Palestinian body politic and national movement, their ties with Syria and Iran have been based on more than mere instrumental subservience or the requirements of survival. For these groups, Syria and Iran represent powerful regional actors whose policy towards the PLO's political and negotiating line adds to the cumulative effect of their opposition and serves to uphold certain Palestinian 'fundamentals' *(thawabit)* such as the right to self-determination and the 'right of return' that might otherwise be diluted or totally lost. The degree to which Syrian–Iranian pressure has actually affected the PLO's decision-making (particularly since the establishment of the PNA) is debatable; except for such groups, the PLO's perceived tendency to make concessions would otherwise remain totally unchecked.

In general terms the PFLP/PDF position has been closely aligned to that of Syria and has followed Syria's lead in calling for a comprehensive settlement based on 'international legitimacy' (e.g. UN Resolution 242) and Arab 'coordination and cooperation' in addressing a settlement. Nonetheless, as part of the complex picture of Palestinian–Syrian relations, both groups were markedly hostile to the US coalition against Saddam during the Gulf war, in sharp contrast to the position of Syria itself, without apparently seriously jeopardizing their relations with Damascus. Ahmad Jibril's PFLP-GC, the secular-nationalist group traditionally most closely associated with Syria, has maintained a consistently hardline approach to the Arab–Israeli conflict that appears in contradiction to the Syrian 'strategic commitment' to a negotiated settlement. But Jibril's hardline approach is also often exploited as a means of putting Syrian pressure on the PLO and other parties and is thus consistent with broader Syrian policy objectives. Jibril has also developed more intimate ties with Iran compared with the PFLP and PDF and has been received regularly in Tehran as part of Iran's ongoing efforts to develop a more active anti-Arafat coalition. The PFLP-GC's political discourse has thus recently undergone a subtle shift towards a more overtly Islamic posture compared with the other two more avowedly Marxist organizations. In the end, however, Jibril, the PFLP and the PDF all have to weigh their position very carefully. Given their current reliance on Syrian political and material support, all three groups appear wary of embarrassing their hosts by operations that could rekindle the issue of Syrian links to 'terrorism'. This is an important consideration in terms of Syria's interest in consolidating its relations with the United States and its readiness to make 'confidence-building' gestures towards Israel.

The position of Hamas and Islamic Jihad is somewhat different. For one thing, the Islamic groups' political and organizational centre of gravity and popular base lie within the Occupied Territories and not in the camps of Lebanon and Syria, as is largely the case with the other secular-nationalist opposition. Unlike the other groups, Hamas and Islamic Jihad have not attempted to carry out any military infiltration across Israel's borders (e.g. from South Lebanon), nor do they maintain external bases for mounting such operations. This does not prevent them from drawing on friendly sources of arms, ammunition or personnel where necessary; for instance, both are known to have obtained support from other Islamic groups in Egypt and elsewhere (including the participation of an Egyptian national in an Islamic Jihad attack in Jerusalem in October 1994). But despite the presence of Fathi Shikkaki in Damascus and the cordial relations between Hamas and Islamic Jihad and Iran, the Damascus–Tehran connection itself, though financially, morally and politically important, does not appear central to either group's ability to act and mobilize in the Palestinian arena. But it is important to note some significant differences between the relationships with Syria and Iran of Hamas on the one hand and of Islamic Jihad on the other. As an offshoot of the Ikhwan Muslimun, Hamas's relations with Syria remain circumscribed to some extent by the brutal struggle for power between the regime and the Syrian Ikhwan in the early 1980s. Hamas's dealings with Iran are also apt to reflect the Ikhwan's Sunni roots, despite the broad measure of politico-ideological empathy between the two sides. By way of contrast, Islamic Jihad's relations with both countries appear less inhibited or problematic. Shikaki's frequent visits to Tehran and his consultations with Rafsanjani, Khamene'i and Ahmad Khomeni, among others, since 1991, indicate a higher degree of intimacy and association with Iran than Hamas enjoys.

From the Syrian point of view, Hamas and Islamic Jihad operations have acted in concert with the actions of Hizbullah to increase pressure on Israel and enhance the position of the Syrian/Iranian-backed opposition at Arafat's expense. The connection to Hamas and the other opposition groups also gives Syria an important channel of influence within the Palestinian arena. But Syria has no real long-term interest in building up or magnifying the influence of Islamic militancy for its own sake. A settlement will reduce the need for a Syrian lever against Israel and to that extent may affect Syrian links with both Hamas and Islamic Jihad, and the overall level of Syrian support for the rejectionists both inside and outside the Palestinian arena. The status of Damascus as a relatively safe haven after a deal between Syria and Israel (and Lebanon) is uncertain, as is the degree to which the groups will be able to maintain a credible Palestinian political role in permanent exile.

Iran's long-term ability to sustain its relations with the Palestinian rejectionists is also uncertain. While some groups (including possibly the PFLP-GC and Islamic Jihad) may be willing to have a Tehran address as opposed to their current base in Damascus, both distance and practical politics could erode the Iranian role in Palestinian affairs. Without any truly solid extension within the Occupied Territories and/or a Palestinian entity, Iranian links to local parties are unlikely to have any major impact, although they may not be dissolved altogether. But Iran could play an increasingly important role in Palestinian diaspora politics, especially among the potentially disaffected and disenfranchised refugees whose aspirations are unlikely to be fully met by any final-status agreement. With the PLO's external institutions and its political presence appearing to be on the wane as a result of financial constraints and the shift in the centre of gravity to the PNA, a political and organizational vacuum may emerge to give Iran a new foothold in the Palestinian diaspora, especially in Lebanon. Thus in early 1994 Iran offered to finance a number of PLO health and welfare institutions in Lebanon then under threat of collapse due to a dearth of funding since the Gulf war. Arafat's response in rushing financial aid to the institutions concerned temporarily staved off the Iranian challenge, but without pre-empting its potential recurrence. The fact that Iran's initiative was prompted by former Arafat Fateh loyalists suggests that there may be fertile soil for a new set of Iranian–Palestinian links outside the traditional ties with the Damascus-based rejectionists. Such ties may also be fostered by the already extant links between Hizbullah and various Palestinian groups in Lebanon (including the tactical alliance between Hizbullah and Arafat himself against Amal during the 1985-6 'war of the camps'). In the end, however, Iran's future role with the Palestinians in Lebanon will be largely determined by Syria's attitude towards and tolerance of such ties – at least as long as Lebanon remains a Syrian zone of influence. No combination of Palestinian rejectionism and Iranian empathy for the Palestinians is likely to be allowed to develop in directions that would challenge Syria's interest in stabilizing the Lebanese arena or seriously undermine a Syrian-sponsored settlement with Israel.

While both Syria and Iran may be considering the impact of a settlement on their relations, neither side is likely to curtail its options in influencing the other parties concerned. Both parties recognize the centrality of the Palestinian role in developments in the process and will maintain their ties with the Palestinian rejectionists accordingly. Iranian–Palestinian links that are facilitated by Syria or that are largely determined by Syrian control on the ground in Lebanon do not necessarily contradict Syrian interests. At the same time the Iranian link to Hizbullah, for instance, serves the vital purpose of distancing Syria from acts of violence against Israel while at the same time allowing it to benefit from the effect of Hizbullah pressure on Israel in the interlocking negotiations over the Lebanese and Syrian tracks. It also distances Damascus from some of the more radical opinions that are voiced by pro-Iranian groups while testing out the reactions of the various parties to such opinions. From the Iranian point of view, much is to be gained in terms of presence and overall freedom of action by supporting the rejectionists and other factions up to the point of Syrian tolerability. In the end, however, and given that Syria is more important to Iran than the rejectionists are, Iran will neither allow the rejectionists to spoil its relationship with Syria nor act independently against Syrian interests. In so far as the Iranian connection with such groups sets a manageable limit on the nature and extent of Palestinian rejectionism, Syria may see this as a facilitating factor in the overall peace process rather than the opposite. It may equally prefer an Iranian link – or final address – for such groups to other possible alternatives such as Iraq or Libya.

Chapter 5

Relations with the United States and Russia

The US factor: a more positive relationship

Syria's and Iran's perceptions of the importance of the US role in the area may be an important determinant of their relations subsequent to an Arab–Israeli settlement. Syria's relations with Iran may increase Western suspicions of Syria, but this relationship also serves to heighten US and Western interest in Syria's role both as a possible modifier of Iranian foreign policy and as a potential indirect channel to Iran. This perception is partly shaped by the role already played by Syria during the various hostage crises in Lebanon and is similar to the sort of role Syria has played for some time between Iran and other Arab countries, particularly the Gulf states. Similarly, Iran's interest in a Syrian connection can be seen as a function of its interest in maintaining informal channels of contact with the United States and the relative credibility and reliability the Syrians may have in this respect compared with other potential conduits from an Iranian point of view.

Offering its good offices to Iran as an intermediary could be a considerable asset to Syria as it builds a new relationship with the United States, and the West generally. Far from discouraging Syrian–Iranian ties as part of the price Syria has to pay for a Middle East settlement, Western interests may lie in precisely the opposite direction, in the exploitation of these ties so as to hold out the promise of improved Western relations with Iran as well as to contain anti-Western Iranian policies where possible. For its part, Iran recognizes the value of such contacts and may seek to encourage Syria's ambitions to play the role of intermediary, a role that carries no particular penalty or risk from an Iranian point of view.

Although it may be premature to speculate about the future of US–Syrian ties after a settlement, it is important to note that a new and more

95

positive relationship has begun to develop between the two countries, including a broad measure of understanding on regional issues and the prospects of more extensive economic relations. This is already shaping up as a result of assiduous US efforts to maintain good relations with Syria, as manifest in two summit meetings so far between Presidents Assad and Clinton including Clinton's politically and symbolically important visit to Damascus in October 1994, which was received with great public satisfaction by the Syrian side. Such US efforts not only serve to facilitate a Syrian–Israeli agreement on the Golan but help to ensure continued Syrian support for US policy towards Iraq, as during the build-up of Iraqi forces against Kuwait in October 1994. Equally important from a Syrian point of view is the fact that current US policy helps to underscore America's appreciation of Syria's regional role and importance as well as its understanding of particular Syrian concerns such as in the Lebanon. In this sense the US policy of dual containment against Iraq and Iran allows Syria a wider margin of manoeuvre with the United States itself and helps Syria to be seen by that country as a regional 'stabilizer' against both Iraq and Iran. The United States may eventually seek to draw Syria into the wider net of pro-Western regional powers but it is unlikely that this will be formalized in any manner (e.g. bilateral defence understandings or joint military manoeuvres), as was the case in agreements made with other parties in the area such as Egypt, Israel or the Arab Gulf countries.

One especial consideration from the Syrian point of view is the prospect of a direct US role in security arrangements on the Golan, where a serious US engagement in both peacemaking and peacekeeping could help to deter Israeli military adventurism and blunt the effect of overall Israeli military superiority on the terms of a settlement. The Syrian approach to negotiations has in fact been predicated upon the assumption of US even-handedness and a high degree of understanding of Syria's own security concerns as well as Israel's. In practical terms, this has been translated into a Syrian interest in US guarantees for any new security regime that may include a US military presence in the Golan as part of a multinational effort similar in intent, if not necessarily in structure, to the force deployed as part of Israeli–Egyptian security arrangements in Sinai. The Clinton administration's readiness to consider such a role has helped to enhance Syrian confidence in US policies, but the advent of a more reticent Republican-dominated Congress with key leaders apparently attuned to right-wing Likud-oriented views on a Golan settlement may pose a significant threat to the current US–Syrian dialogue. This in turn is likely to complicate and delay both the pace of Israeli–Syrian negotiations and the chances of a further improvement in Syrian–US ties. Without a US security guarantee of one form or another on the Golan, Syria's readiness to respond to Israel's security requirements may diminish, as may the prospects for an early breakthrough on the entire Golan package.

US troops on the Golan – in whatever guise – are unlikely to be welcome in Tehran, given the long-standing Iranian opposition to any Western military presence in the area, and any eventual agreement on such a deployment may face criticism from the Iranians, as indeed may any overall Israeli–Syrian peace accord. Nonetheless, Iran is unlikely to consider a US presence on the Golan as constituting any significant threat to Iran itself; its reactions are likely to be limited, given its relatively muted response to a potentially much more problematic build-up of US forces in the Gulf, where, unlike on the Golan, vital Iranian interests are at stake. Iran's ability to oppose Syria in this respect will also be circumscribed by the total control Syria exerts over the arena and the seriousness with which it is likely to view any Iranian challenge there. In any event, a negative Iranian response to the notion of a US presence on the Golan will not be sufficient to deter Syria from pursuing its vital national interests here, especially where such a presence may be linked, from a Syrian point of view, to both the long-term stability of the peace arrangements with Israel and a quantum leap in future US–Syrian political and economic relations.

Barring a serious US–Syrian rift in the near future over the terms of a settlement with Israel or other regional issues (Lebanon, Iraq, etc.), there is no reason to assume that Syria cannot maintain a good working relationship with the United States for the foreseeable future. This is not to preclude differences arising out of possible Syrian tensions with Turkey, or post-Saddam Iraq, or Israel, subsequent to a settlement. One source of tension could be US support for new regional configurations such as Israel-Jordan-Iraq or Israel-Egypt-Turkey. Another could be an escalating US campaign against Iran after an Arab–Israeli settlement. In the short term at least, Syria is likely to resist any US attempts to pressure it into some more active variant of dual containment, which it may see as forcing it to choose between its alliance with Iran and a policy that merges Iran and Saddam into one common threat. Other things being equal, Syrian interests dictate maintaining an equidistant relationship between Washington and Tehran such that it would not have to sacrifice its ties with one in favour of the other. A Syrian stance based on good relations with the West but without any clear identification with Western policies in the area will allow Syria to maintain its association with Iran (and vice versa) with minimum embarrassment and maximum utility for all parties concerned. It would also be consistent with Syria's long-standing politico-ideological posture and its own perception of its Arab and regional roles.

A complicating factor arises from growing US–Iranian tensions. Contrary to expectations, the escalation of US efforts to boycott trade and investment with Iran may paradoxically increase the challenges faced by the Arab–Israeli peace process: if sanctions against Iraq are not lifted and the prospects of both an Iraqi–Israeli and an Iraqi–American dialogue recede, then the chances of a more *effective* Iranian–Iraqi rapprochement may be strengthened. This would potentially create a formidable focus for opposition forces to the process. Furthermore, and in the absence of any significant progress on the Syrian–Israeli track, Syria may become more susceptible to Iranian rejectionist pressures. While Iranian opposition to the peace process and to Syria's participation in the negotiations has been largely verbal so far, Iran's perceptions of a US-led offensive against it may push it to pursue more active forms of opposition. With Libya as another potential partner, the formation of a new regional alignment of forces in active opposition to a settlement may thus be the inadvertent result of the current US stance against Iran.

The Russian factor: a limited role

Prior to its demise, the Soviet Union was an important element in Syrian–Iranian relations. Syria's role as a conduit for Soviet arms to Iran during the initial phases of the Gulf war (up to 1982) was but one aspect of the trilateral relationship, allowing both the Syrians and the Soviet Union to support Iran without any direct responsibility and involvement in the war. All three parties have also benefited from Syria's readiness to act as an indirect political channel between Tehran and Moscow. Syria's bilateral relations with the Soviet Union were a vital strategic asset throughout the Cold War and a central plank of Syria's defence posture against Israel. For Iran, the Soviet Union was similarly an implicit though inconstant counterbalance to the greater external enemy, the United States. Geostrategic factors such as proximity and the need for stability on Iran's northern borders, as well as the imperatives of trade, kept Iranian–Soviet relations on a relatively even keel despite Iran's official revilement of both superpowers, differences with the Soviet Union over the Iranian communist Tudeh party and the eventual Soviet tilt towards Iraq after 1982.

The collapse of the Soviet Union in 1991 was instrumental in a number of vital changes in Syria's political posture. These included the virtual abandonment of the military struggle against Israel, as codified in the Syrian doctrine of 'strategic parity', and the Syrian commitment to the Madrid process, leading to the development of much-improved relations with the United States. During the first half of the 1990s Syrian policy has in fact been predicated on the assumption of a unipolar world with the United States as supreme arbiter, at least as far as Arab–Israeli and Middle Eastern issues are concerned. Consequently, Syrian–Russian relations and Arab–Russian relations generally have been substantially downgraded in comparison with those that previously existed with the Soviet Union. This has reflected Moscow's own weaknesses and preoccupations as well as its apparent readiness to let Washington dominate the post-Madrid negotiating and diplomatic processes on the Arab–Israeli front. The Russo-Iranian relationship, by contrast, has not been substantially altered by the collapse of the Soviet Union. The strategic advantages gained by Iran from the disappearance of the Soviet military and ideological threat have been largely counterbalanced by a new sense of vulnerability resulting from an assertive US doctrine of containment and a new Western military profile in the area after the Gulf war. Events on Iran's northern borders have also tended to replace a relatively stable Soviet control with a proliferation of 'northern tier' uncertainties. Nonetheless, a balance seems to have been found between Russia's concerns regarding Iranian intervention or Iranian-backed Islamic activism in Azerbaijan and Tajikistan and elsewhere along the Russian southern perimeter and Iranian interest in access to Russian arms and trade. Indeed, Iranian policy since 1991 has been marked by considerable caution in dealing with events in the former southern republics of the Soviet Union. This caution stems from a desire to maintain a tolerable level of mutual goodwill with Moscow as well as to avoid direct friction and competition with Turkey – or, conversely, any sense of alignment with Turkey against Russia. Finally, Tehran has a clear interest in avoiding any spillover effect from local conflicts into Iran itself, given the underlying political and ethnic complexities in the area – an interest underlined by Tehran's surprising forbearance regarding Russia's 'anti-Muslim' policy in Chechenia and Bosnia.

The period of relative Russian quiescence in the Middle East may, however, be coming to an end. Driven by economic needs as well as strategic imperatives, a more active and independent Russian policy that is distinct and separate from the previous alignment with the United States may be taking shape on a number of levels. Most significant for both Syria and Iran is the current Russian pressure for the international rehabilitation of Iraq. Russia has put itself forward not only as an international intermediary on Iraq's behalf (as witnessed by the successive visits of Iraqi ministers and emissaries to Moscow since 1991) but as an independent crisis manager in regional conflict. Russian foreign minister Andrei Kozyrev's mission to Baghdad and the Gulf during the 1994 Kuwait crisis was intended as a demonstration of diplomatic skill as much as a message that Russia still considers itself to be a major world power with special interests in the area. In spite of the limited Russian success in this instance (although a formal Iraqi commitment to the recognition of Kuwait cannot be considered as entirely incidental), the prospect of revived and reinvigorated Russian–Iraqi relations must be a matter of concern for Syria and Iran. If Russia and other parties such as France can ultimately succeed in lifting the sanctions regime, Iraq – and Saddam – could well re-emerge on the regional scene with powerful external allies potentially ready to support the redevelopment of the Iraqi economy and capable of supplying Iraqi forces with a new set of modern arms and weapons systems. Although a free flow of Russian arms to Iraq may not materialize immediately after an end to the sanctions regime, neither Syria nor Iran can afford to ignore the implications of such an eventuality.

The possible development of Iraqi–Russian relations is likely to add to Syria's and Iran's incentives to maintain their relationship for the foreseeable future. Even without Saddam, a Russian-backed militarily and economically resurgent Iraq is a problematic prospect for both countries. But Russia's opening to Iraq has been matched by other recent Russian moves in the area: in its new diplomatic activism Russia has attempted to create balanced relationships with all the major regional actors. Russian links in the Gulf have been consolidated by a bilateral defence pact with Kuwait (similar in form to those between Kuwait and the major Western allies) and Russia has aggressively promoted its new military technologies with the GCC states. Russian–Israeli ties have transformed the former antagonisms of the Soviet era into comparatively warm and flourishing political and economic relations. The first ever visit of an Israeli prime minister to Moscow in spring 1994 was the occasion of a reported offer from Yeltsin to Rabin of a joint agreement on defence production in addition to the agreed trade protocol initialled during the visit. The Russian–Israeli consultations also touched upon the issues of 'Islamic extremism' and Iranian policy in Central Asia, as well as Russian arms sales in the Middle East and Israel's wish to restrain possible Russian military supplies to Syria and Iran.

It is worth noting, however, that Rabin's Moscow visit coincided with a high-level Russian mission to Syria. Russian military sales to Syria were only partially affected by the demise of the Soviet Union, and after a hiatus between 1992 and 1994 Russia's traditional role as a major arms supplier to Syria appears to have been reinstated. Given that some 90 per cent of Syrian military equipment is of Soviet origin, the apparent loss of the USSR as a source of arms after 1991 and the lack of any reliable major substitute supplier faced Syria with the distinct danger of a substantial degradation of its military power over the next few years. The re-establishment of Russian–Syrian military ties will thus have partly assuaged major Syrian concerns regarding the wholesale obsolescence of its Soviet-supplied equipment and the credibility of its defence posture.

The effect of Syria's acquisition of new Russian arms on the Syrian–Israeli relationship and the negotiations on the Golan is likely to be limited. As long as Syria's political commitment to a settlement holds, this renewed Russian link is unlikely to change the balance of power or deflect the process, although it may act to harden Syria's position in any negotiations on security arrangements with Israel. For its part, Russia has to balance against the political and economic benefits of renewed military ties with Syria the negative effect this may have on its budding relations with Israel. The likelihood of a full-scale Russian political or military alliance with Israel remains weak, given the nature and extent of US–Israeli ties; but Russia's ability to move relatively freely across the Arab–Israeli divide may present new diplomatic opportunities for a more active Russian role. This was manifest in Kozyrev's mission to Tel Aviv in mid-1994 with a view to calling a 'Madrid-2' conference as a means of revitalizing the Middle East peace process. Though ill-conceived and received coolly at the time by Israel and the United States (not by Syria or the PLO), this initiative may pave the way for a somewhat more carefully considered Russian initiative in the future.

Russian arms sales and trade with Syria have run parallel to a similar relationship with Iran. The major Iranian breakthrough in this respect was the fruit of President Rafsanjani's visit to Moscow in May 1989 before the collapse of the Soviet Union, resulting in a $15 billion trade agreement, of which $4 billion was reportedly for arms. For both Syria and Iran, Russian arms supplies serve a number of important politico-military purposes. First, they include major high-technology systems (aircraft, tanks, ground-to-air missiles) that are otherwise difficult to obtain on the world market. Neither China nor North Korea is currently or in the short to medium term capable of producing advanced major weapon systems to match their Western counterparts in service with potential protagonists such as Israel and Iraq (in the case of Syria or Iran) or the United States and Saudi Arabia (in the case of Iran alone). Second, Russian arms enhance the prospects of Syrian–Iranian military collaboration by creating a relatively wide base of common equipment and military stockpiles. While Syrian and Iranian acquisition of Scud-Cs from North Korea has apparently led to cooperation between the two countries on a Scud production line in Syria itself, Russian supplies cover a wider range of *matériel*, and may be of greater multipurpose value in a crisis, such as for mutually supportive rapid deployment, or in times of war, as was the case with Syrian supplies to Iran during the Iran–Iraq war. Third, while there is little evidence that arms and trade alone constitute sufficient means of influencing the overall stance or policies of the supplier (or of the recipient, for that matter), Syria and Iran may hope to use their military relations with Russia as a way of modifying Russian policy in areas of common interest.

Other factors also affect Syrian–Iranian relations with Russia. For both countries, Russia can play an important balancing role *vis-à-vis* other regional players, particularly Turkey. Strong Syrian relations with Russia could help to contain Turkish freedom of action with Israel or in the Arab arena at large. For its part, Iran has a long-standing interest in maintaining Russian leverage against Turkish Central Asian 'expansionism' or as a means of curtailing a more active Turkish role in the Gulf. Of particular, perhaps vital, interest to Iran is the oil factor. Since the Iranian revolution, Iran's stance towards the Soviet Union/Russia has been substantially determined by the desire to secure a share of the enormous economic potential of oil pipelines through Russia and/or other former Soviet territories. This has led to a measure of competition between Russia and Iran over the alternative possible routes for such pipelines and friction over the development of Azeri offshore fields in the Caspian Sea. One measure of the complexity of Iranian–Russian relations is that such competition has to be set against the development of significant joint ventures and interests, including a Russian commitment to help in the revitalization of Iran's moribund nuclear energy programme. In January 1995 a Russian–Iranian deal to supply Iran's nuclear facility at Bushehr with two 440 MW reactors was concluded after some years of negotiations. Over and above the financial aspects of this deal (initially estimated at some $800 million), there may be some Russian interest in setting support for Iran's nuclear energy programme against Russo-Iranian competition over oil pipelines.

Such interests aside, there are limitations on any new Russian activist role in conjunction with either Syria or Iran. From a Syrian point of view, close relations with an 'activist' Russia may have a cost in terms of US confidence in Syria itself. So long as Syria aims to ensure both the continuation of US sponsorship of the peace process and the prospects of improved US–Syrian economic ties after a settlement, it is unlikely that it will allow its relationship with Russia to impinge on its relations with the United States. This does not entirely preclude Syrian attempts to utilize its Russian connection to exert some pressure on the United States, but it does militate against any full-scale alignment with Russia against the United States, were such a polarization to reappear in the short to medium term. Syrian policy could change in this respect in the event of a serious breakdown in the peace process, or if the United States were to pull out of its current commitments (as understood in Damascus) or adopt a hostile attitude towards Syria for other reasons (e.g. 'sponsorship of terrorism'). In the end, however, the Russian ability to deliver on both the political and the military fronts will remain limited and will be seen as such in Damascus and Tehran for some time to come at least. Russia's internal instability, economic weakness and perceived lack of politico-diplomatic consistency will limit both Syria's belief in the possibility of reviving a strategic relationship along the lines of the former relationship with the Soviet Union and Iranian reliance on Russia as an effective counterbalance to the United States.

Chapter 6

Military, economic and domestic factors

Military cooperation and interests

Syrian–Iranian military relations remain subject to speculation, given the absence of official confirmation by either side of the nature and extent of military and defence cooperation between them. Western, Israeli and Iraqi sources have nonetheless consistently suggested that the alliance has involved military cooperation on several levels, ranging from the trans-shipment of third-party arms and equipment to the co-production of weapon systems. Other elements of this cooperation, such as operational coordination in the logistical supply and back-up for proxy forces and allied elements such as the Palestinian rejectionist groups and Pasdaran and Hizbullah forces in Lebanon, have equally remained unannounced, although some aspects have on occasion been confirmed by the Iranian side.

During President Assad's visit to Moscow for the signature of the Syrian–Soviet Friendship and Cooperation Treaty as early as October 1980, one month after the outbreak of the Iran–Iraq war, Syria reportedly interceded on Iran's behalf in order to facilitate Soviet arms shipments to Tehran and the despatch of additional supplies direct from Syria and Libya. Starting in November 1980, Syrian airspace and ports were also used to maintain a flow of Arab arms to Iran, including the first shipment of Scud-B missiles from Libya and other arms from Algeria by mid-1981. These supplies were backed by a Syrian military training and assistance mission to Iran and by increased Syrian aid to the Kurdish insurgency against the Iraqi regime. The March 1982 Syrian–Iranian oil and trade agreement marked the first formalization of the alliance and is also reported to have included additional Syrian arms supplies to Iran as well as an unconfirmed deployment of Syrian troops to Iraq's borders to coincide with the closure of the Iraqi–Syrian pipeline in April 1982. After mid-1982, Syria's preoccupation with the Israeli threat in Lebanon and its reservations towards the Iranian pursuit of the war into Iraqi territory appear to have precluded any further significant military aid to Iran. Little evidence exists of any subsequent shipment of Syrian arms or troop deployments in support of Iran until the end of the Iran–Iraq war in 1988, although there are some suggestions of Syrian technical assistance with the operation of Iranian Scud-B missiles obtained from Libya as late as 1985.

The net effect of Syrian arms supplies to Iran during the Iran–Iraq war is difficult to gauge. By and large the evidence points to a limited strategic impact, although Syrian arms may have played an important role in sustaining the Iranian war effort and providing technical and logistical assistance at a time when few external sources were available to Tehran. By the mid-1980s Iran had turned to alternative sources and the bulk of its arms acquisitions came from China, North Korea and other secondary suppliers in Eastern Europe and elsewhere. This pattern has been maintained since, with new supplies obtained directly from the Soviet Union/Russia and China in the late 1980s and 1990s forming the basis of Iran's current modernization programme. Set in perspective, past Syrian military shipments to Iran – whatever their true extent – appear to have had no significant impact on the defence capabilities of the Islamic Republic and can no longer be considered a major element in the overall relationship between the two sides.

Common security interests do, however, continue to affect this relationship. Both Syria and Iran have developed a similar requirement for a ballistic missile capability, and have faced similar difficulties in obtaining access to such weapon systems and the requisite technology. The Iran–Iraq 'war of the cities' in 1988, which saw the pounding of Iranian urban centres by some 200 Iraqi-modified Scud-B missiles, left the Iranians with around 10,000 civilian casualties and a deep sense of vulnerability, as well as a strong incentive to build a deterrent force that would prevent the recurrence of such a threat. On the Syrian side, the long-standing strategic threat posed by the Israeli airforce – amply demonstrated in 1973 and 1982 – and Israel's own missile capabilities have provided a commensurate rationale for the development of a deterrent capability that would limit Israel's freedom of action and raise the cost of an Israeli military initiative against Syria. While Syria succeeded in obtaining Scud-Bs from the Soviet Union after 1974 and the more accurate but shorter range SS-21s after 1982, Soviet/Russian reluctance to upgrade Syria's tactical missile force since the late 1980s has led it to turn to other sources; and after Iran's limited supply of Scud-Bs was effectively exhausted during the war with Iraq, the need to replenish and develop its missile stock also became pressing.

Persistent US attempts to contain ballistic missile proliferation in the Third World, with a special emphasis on preventive measures against Syria and Iran coupled with Soviet/Russian readiness to abide by the Missile Technology Control Regime (MTCR), have left two primary sources of tactical and intermediate-range missiles open to the alliance: North Korea and China. Starting in 1991 Syria is reported to have taken delivery of North Korean Scud-Cs with a 500 km range, compared with the 290 km range of the Soviet-supplied Scud-B. This deal was apparently negotiated in coordination with a similar Iranian request for this missile, and the first delivery of North Korean Scud-Cs to Iran was made in 1992. The sale of Chinese missiles to either country remains unconfirmed, although there have been reports of a deal for M9 missiles (with a 600 km range) to Syria since 1987. Chinese adherence to the MTCR in 1992 may have blocked the deal, and by mid-1994 Israeli sources were suggesting that no direct deliveries had so far been made. For its part, North Korea has supplied Iran with Scud-C missiles and has apparently been negotiating a deal for the supply of the more advanced Nodung-1 (Scud-D) with a 1,000 km range since the early 1990s. Israeli efforts to block such a deal included a brief opening to North Korea in 1992–3, with a view to offering Israeli trade and a channel to the United States as incentives against the purported deal. Although the Israeli initiative has had no evident results on a bilateral level, largely due to US dissatisfaction with Israel's unilateral action, no deliveries of Nodung-1 missiles to Iran had been confirmed by 1994.

The difficulties and uncertainties surrounding the direct delivery of missiles from China and North Korea appear to have led to the adoption by Syria and Iran of a different option. Western and Israeli sources report that North Korea and Iran have been collaborating on a local assembly line for Scud-C missiles in Syria at two facilities near Aleppo and Hama. Components for this production line have been shipped to Syria via Iran and test firings have taken place in both countries. Other unconfirmed reports suggest that China may also be helping to set up installations for the production of solid-fuel missiles in Syria and/or a seperate M9 facility with Iranian technical assistance. Over the past few years Iran itself has announced the development of a number of locally designed missiles, including one with a range of 800 km in 1989. In view of Iran's indigenous missile programme, its interest in assisting a separate production capability in Syria is not self-evident. One reason may be a desire to secure a back-up resource, with the Syrian-based facility providing an additional source in time of need. Equally, the Iranian perception may be that a Syrian-based facility would be more secure in the case of a renewal of the conflict with Iraq or other parties. Technical reasons or the political requirements of the external parties may also be involved, given that the transfer of technology is generally less transparent than transfers of the complete weapon systems themselves. From a Syrian point of view, Iran's technological base, its possible financial support and its role as an alternative route for the acquisition of component parts, as well as its experience during the war with Iraq, may all provide useful inputs into a local missile production programme. One offshoot of this collaboration may be some advanced technology projects such as a reported joint effort to develop cruise missiles in 1993, with technology coming from Europe and Japan. Although this report was strongly denied by Iran, Syrian–Iranian collaboration may increase the combined access to Western and other technology not easily obtainable by either party acting on its own. The EC's 1994 decision to lift the arms embargo on Syria may provide one such example, although Syria's fears of losing such access may equally deter it from sharing any acquisitions with Iran.

Syrian–Iranian cooperative efforts in the field of missile technology make some sense in the light of both countries' efforts to develop long-range delivery systems with non-conventional warheads. Unlike Iran, Syria's interest in the nuclear field remains limited, as does its interest in the development of other types of non-conventional weaponry such as biological weapons. While Syrian–Iranian cooperation in these areas remains possible, little evidence exists to support the view that it is a current priority for either side. Syria is, however, reported to have a relatively advanced chemical warhead programme, while the Iranian chemical programme remains rudimentary by comparison. This may provide grounds for collaboration on chemical warheads in tandem with the joint development of ballistic missiles. A credible non-conventional capability in chemical weapons rests at the heart of Syrian efforts to match and at least partly neutralize Israeli nuclear superiority as well as to limit the rising ceiling of Israeli conventional superiority. With operational Scud-Cs, Syria's deterrent/retaliatory reach extends from the Syrian heartland southwards to cover the whole of Israel, northwards to central Turkey and eastwards to Iraq and northern Saudi Arabia. While other elements of Syrian force projection such as the Su-24 attack aircraft can already reach beyond this range to Egypt, Kuwait and the Caspian Sea, the combination of comparative invulnerability and cost-effectiveness gives the Syrian missile force (reportedly one of the largest in the Third World today) a particular potency. Syrian interest in such a force is thus likely to extend beyond direct confrontation with Israel and a possible settlement on the Golan. In a post-settlement environment Syria may have to contend with new sources of threat, including a resurgent and hostile Iraq; and it will perceive its long-range missile and chemical warhead capability as a continued deterrent against both Iraq and Israel even after a settlement, especially in view of Israel's determination to maintain its nuclear capability and continued fears regarding Iraq's capabilities and intentions in this respect. Syrian force projection will also be seen to support its stance *vis-à-vis* Turkey and will add to its weight as a regional power in the Mediterranean, inter-Arab and Gulf domains. Similarly, Iran's chemical and missile capability as well as its nuclear programme will strengthen Iranian deterrence against Iraq, especially in view of Iraq's record of chemical attacks during the Iran–Iraq war and the possible reactivation of its nuclear activities. Iranian power projection via its ballistic missiles must also be seen in the context of its strategic concerns regarding the Central Asian republics, Russia, Turkey, Afghanistan, Pakistan and the Gulf states. An additional incentive for both parties has been the proliferation of ballistic missiles within the Middle East arena, including Iraq, Saudi Arabia and Israel, and the likelihood that this will not be seriously checked in the short term at least.

Syrian interests may not preclude the maintenance of Iranian–Israeli tensions in the pre-settlement phase. Syria's alliance with Iran adds to the uncertainties of any future Syrian–Israeli conflict should the peace process collapse. Such tensions also add to the planning and operational burdens of the Israeli side, regardless of the actual likelihood of joint or separate Syrian–Iranian actions in such a conflict. For the same reasons, the alliance equally helps to bolster Syrian confidence during the negotiations. But a Syrian–Israeli settlement complete with security arrangements, limited force zones and early warning systems, guaranteed by the United States and bound by a mutual commitment to end the use of force, will necessarily preclude an active Iranian role against Israel from Syrian territory. Indeed, given that such a role has not been requested in the past, it is as unlikely that Syria will solicit such a role as it is that Iran will seek to impose it against Syria's interest and will after a settlement.

Iraq's nuclear potential should be seen as a primary Iranian strategic concern and one that significantly motivates its own non-conventional efforts across the board. Unlike Syria, Iran also has to contend with a broader nuclear environment in Central and Southeast Asia, including China, India and Pakistan. At the same time, Israeli–Iranian tensions over Iran's nuclear programme may continue to escalate, as may Israeli–US concerns about Iran's long-range missile capabilities. With the possible acquisition of longer-range missiles such as the Nodung-1 or even a cruise missile capability, Iran's strategic reach may well extend to Israel in the short to medium term. Paired with the possible acceleration of its nuclear programme (despite widely differing US and Israeli views on its real nuclear capabilities and timetable), Iran's ability to pose a separate non-conventional threat to Israel, outside the context of its alliance with Syria, cannot be ruled out as a matter of principle. In practice, however, the Iranian incentive actively to pursue such a threat is unclear. Ideological opposition to Israel aside, the material and political costs of any direct military initiative against Israel will be apparent in Tehran. From an Iranian perspective Israel's own unsafeguarded and unrestricted nuclear programme, coupled with periodic threats to take 'pre-emptive measures' against Iranian nuclear facilities, are sufficient evidence of Israel's hostile intentions and thus credible grounds for developing an Iranian counter-deterrent. Since 1980 Iran has shown no clear commitment to a direct military confrontation with Israel and will most probably continue to shy away from such a commitment as long as there is no perceived direct threat to Iranian security from Israel itself. Furthermore, an Iranian–Israeli conflict that occurs in the context of a comprehensive Middle East settlement will make it difficult for any Arab party, including Syria, to offer Iran significant military aid.

The past history of the Syrian–Iranian relationship and the divergent strategic priorities of the two countries suggest that their future military cooperation will not involve any significant deployments of troops or large-scale direct participation in either side's conflicts with third parties, except in exceptional circumstances. This does not deny the possibility of a common approach to conflicts where both have similar or overlapping interests. One arena which may be the occasion of joint action is Iraq. A future Iraqi assault on either party may revive some of the elements of their cooperation during the Iran–Iraq war, with the extent of this depending on the prevailing regional and international circumstances. A post-Saddam Iraqi–Iranian or Syrian–Iraqi conflict, for instance, may well elicit a different reaction from one initiated by a resurgent Saddam. Both Syria and Iran may also consider extending their combined security efforts to confront future Iraqi actions in the Gulf (against Kuwait for instance) if such actions were to coincide with their own Gulf interests or those of the Gulf states themselves. Other local conflicts, such as a future Syrian–Turkish clash, may be more problematic; but the alliance may still have an effect on third parties, as a means of compulsion or as an indirect means of deterrence through uncertainty.

In the short term, however, Syria and Iran are most likely to continue their cooperation in supporting proxy forces against Israel, particularly in South Lebanon, although a Syrian–Lebanese settlement with Israel may shift the focus of such action to other fronts such as oppositional forces in Iraq. Common threat perceptions will equally ensure that Syria and Iran continue efforts to develop their deterrent capabilities, partly against Israel, partly against Iraq and partly as a means of strengthening their security overall. In this respect, the main focus of their joint activities may remain that of research and development in fields such as missile and non-conventional technologies that yield a common dividend at relatively low risk and without any necessary commitment to common action against third-party threats.

The economic arena

Given that the alliance was initially founded on an economic and trade agreement, economic factors have clearly played an important role in the Syrian–Iranian relationship. The close interplay between strategic, military and economic factors is also highlighted by the apparent linkage between Iranian oil deliveries to Syria and Syrian military assistance and political support for Iran in the war against Iraq. Other subsequent non-oil bilateral trade agreements made during the early to mid-1980s were probably perceived by both sides as a useful means to sustain the alliance and create a common network of interests.

In the first phases of the alliance Syria benefited from Iranian oil and financial aid (through deferred payments for oil) at a time when the Syrian economy was facing increasing difficulties. As early as 1980 Iran began to supply Syria with discounted oil. The 1982 and later agreements codified Iran's readiness to provide Syria with discounted crude oil in exchange for various goods, including phosphates and industrial products as well as arms. An agreement in April 1983 included the supply of one million tonnes of crude oil free of charge to the Syrian army for the 'continuation of the struggle against Zionism'. The amounts of discounted and gratis oil supplies varied through the period 1984–8 depending on the state of the Iranian economy and its production capabilities, which were increasingly affected by Iraqi air strikes as the war dragged on. Iran's readiness to provide Syria with oil also varied depending on the state of bilateral political relations: deliveries were suspended in early 1986 owing to differences over Lebanon, but as late as 1987 the Syrian army was still officially the annual beneficiary of 300,000 tonnes of free crude oil. In April 1987 Iranian supplies were once again renewed at a rate of one million tonnes annually gratis and additional supplies at market prices. But as Iranian oil supplies became increasingly problematic for Iran itself owing to a combination of war damage and some internal resentment at the sacrifices that were seen to be made on Syria's behalf, Syria's own local production of oil began to rise. By the end of the Gulf war, it had begun to provide a viable alternative to Iranian and other externally supplied oil.

From a Syrian point of view Iranian oil supplies were beneficial at a number of levels. Access to free oil, particularly for the Syrian army, must have significantly helped to defray Syrian costs in Lebanon, estimated to have reached around $1 million a day in the early 1980s. Equally, spiralling defence costs throughout the 1980s placed an enormous burden on the Syrian economy, leading to a severe economic crisis and a 5 per cent drop in GNP in 1986. This coincided with a decline of Arab financial aid from the Gulf states, by then deeply committed to financing Saddam's war against Iran, and rising pressures on Syria to repay its considerable debt to the Soviet Union. Free and discounted oil from Iran, and Iranian forbearance in demanding repayments (with a $1.2 billion debt for previous oil shipments rescheduled by the Majlis in 1987) may have been a crucial economic boon at a time of crisis.

Syrian trade relations with Iran have included other elements besides oil. Throughout the Iran–Iraq war years bilateral trade agreements included provisions for Syrian exports to Iran of phosphate, linen, cotton, fertilizers, spices, cement, chemicals and electrical appliances. Iranian exports envisaged in these agreements included fisheries, dates, household goods, chemicals, buses, electrical motors and pistachio nuts. A direct air link between Tehran and Damascus was established in 1981, and collaboration on road, sea and rail transport was codified in a series of agreements between 1985 and 1988. The exchange of scientific expertise was agreed in 1983 and collaboration in technical and developmental projects in 1986. Cultural exchanges and offices have been set up in Tehran and Damascus, and media cooperation was agreed in 1985. One important aspect of the relationship has been the visits of Iranian pilgrims and tourists to Syria and in particular to the holy shrine of Sitt-Zienab, the granddaughter of the Prophet Muhammad and the Imam Hussein's daughter Raqiyah in Damascus. During the war with Iraq, visits to these and other sites by Iranian war widows, orphans and crippled soldiers were subsidized jointly by the Syrian and Iranian government as a form of rest and recreation, and as a substitute for the inaccessible Shia shrines in Iraq. By the mid-1980s around 150,000 Iranian tourists were visiting Syria annually. In 1987 agreement was reached on a figure of 2,000 Iranian tourist visits a week. The net result was a considerable Iranian expenditure in Syrian souks and cities (and some individual propensity to private enterprise in street trade among the visitors themselves). At the same time, however, over-zealous Khomeinist sloganeering among Iranian visitors has on occasion been a cause for (minor) friction with the Syrian authorities, and the sharp contrast between Syrian/Sunni 'secularism' and the Shiite orthodoxy of the Iranian regime has not always helped to bridge the cultural gap between the two sides.

By 1992 Syrian oil production at approximately 560,000 barrels/day was over double its level some ten years earlier, at the time of the initial economic and trade agreement with Iran. Since then the Syrian economy has bounced back as a result of some effective government measures, including a growing commitment to a free-market economy, as exemplified by Investment Law no. 10, passed in 1991 which lifted restrictions on private-sector and foreign investment in areas previously reserved for the public sector. Syrian self-sufficiency in oil and the current export of around two-thirds of its oil production have mitigated the need for continued free Iranian supplies, which have been discontinued since 1988–9. Conversely, the end of the Iran–Iraq war has removed the need for any special Iranian treatment of Syria in the economic domain. The relative decline in the importance of the economic factor in the alliance has not, however, had any measurable effect on its overall solidity, which is sustained by a broader coincidence of interests; the current absence of any significant economic basis for the alliance only highlights its ability to adapt to changing circumstances. So long as there is no direct conflict of economic interests and no form of economic dependency by one side on the other, with consequent tensions in the relationship, there is little reason to believe that this will change in the foreseeable future.

The domestic factor: some uncertainties

The Syrian–Iranian alliance has proved to be largely immune to the conflicting internal pressures within each country since the early 1980s.

The fundamental differences in structure, ideology and political belief between the two regimes have so far had no significant impact on the durability of the alliance, despite state-to-state tensions and differences that have occasionally surfaced over Lebanon, the peace process and other issues. However, the possibility of a serious future split in the alliance as a result of potentially discordant *domestic* pressures cannot be excluded altogether.

Iran's competing centres of power may yet produce a shift in the direction of its relationship with Syria. As the struggle for power in Tehran continues, the common ground that has held regarding the overall utility of the alliance since the early 1980s may give way to a more reticent approach, particularly in the event of a wholesale ideological retrenchment away from the pragmatic policies of the current leadership. The apparent absence of a clear locus of decision-making or centralized control over the various strands of the relationship with Syria compounds the difficulty of judging possible future Iranian foreign policy trends, but it is evident that a certain opposition to the prevailing approach to the alliance with Syria exists at a number of levels. Thus debates within the Majlis have suggested that parliamentary support for the relationship with Syria has not been unanimous and that a certain resistance to the alliance has persisted among the more conservative political circles in Iran over the years. Members of the Majlis opposed to the relationship with Syria and the terms of Iranian oil deliveries delayed the ratification of the March 1982 oil and trade agreement until February 1983, and the Iranian decision to renew the oil supply agreement in May 1985 was criticized by several members on the grounds of Syrian delays in payment and Syrian clashes with Islamic forces in Lebanon. As late as November 1992 a government bill proposing an agreement on police cooperation and extradition arrangements between the two countries was opposed on the grounds that the Syrian position regarding Iran 'and the problems of the area' was unsound and was opportunistically based on its hostility towards Iraq rather than any real friendship with Iran. Another criticism was based on the costs that Iran had borne in supporting Syria, including the aid that was 'poured' into the latter's coffers. In supporting the bill and the alliance with Syria, other members recalled Syria's blockage of the Iraqi oil pipeline in 1982 and stressed Iran's interests in Lebanon, while questioning the wisdom and viability of a foreign policy that 'expected Syria to become an Islamic Republic of Iran'. A governmental intervention at this stage stressed the brotherly relations with Syria and the need to expect 'any country to take into account its own interests in its [foreign] political relations'. Although the bill was eventually passed, the debate seems to point to a certain unease within some Iranian political circles over 'normal' dealings with a country that may be exploiting its relations with Iran to its own advantage with material costs but no evident returns from the Iranian point of view.

Other evidence of internal dissension regarding Syria has come from the ultra-religious establishment and has centred on the role and posture of the Iranian foreign ministry, which is generally recognized to reflect President Rafsanjani's pragmatic line. One clear example relates to the criticism of the foreign ministry's relative forbearance regarding the Arab–Israeli peace process and the Syrian participation in the negotiations since Madrid. While in early 1994 foreign minister Velayati explicitly declared that Iran 'would not quarrel with Syria or end its relationship with it' as a result of differences over the peace process, such apparent moderation has found little favour among the centres of power associated with the radical line. When the Iranian ambassador to Bonn was reported in September 1994 to have suggested that Iran 'did not oppose the peace settlement or the Jewish people' and that it could not take a stronger stance than that of the Arab parties themselves, the foreign ministry came in for a harsh critique from *The Islamic Republic*, a radical Tehran daily aligned with Iran's spiritual leader Khamene'i. The newspaper castigated the foreign ministry's 'clear and unequivocal contradiction' of the injunctions issued by Khamene'i and suggested that this was part of a deliberate campaign by the administration to ignore the spiritual leadership's directives.

The specific case against Syria has been taken up in detail elsewhere. A private study published in Iran in early 1994 by Hizbullah-Qom, an influential clerical group led by Hojatolislam Baqer Kharrazi, argued that an Israeli–Syrian agreement is 'inevitable' and that an Arab–Israeli settlement will lead to the 'loss of Palestine and Jerusalem and the abandonment of Muslim interests'. The study also predicted a deterioration in relations with Damascus and a contraction of Iranian influence in the Middle East, including Lebanon, in the aftermath of a breakthrough on the Israeli–Syrian track. In addition it foresaw a post-settlement competition for leadership of the Arab world between Syria and Egypt, with the former exerting influence over Iraq, Jordan and Lebanon and seeking to crush Hizbullah and 'wipe out Iran's bridges with the Lebanese Islamic and nationalist forces for good'. The Qom report suggested that Iran should prepare for these eventualities by seeking new

relations and alliances in the area, without making any specific recom-
mendations in this respect.

Such views among the radical tendency in Tehran have so far been
largely kept in check by Iranian official state policy and the consistency
of President Rafsanjani's own views on the need to maintain the alliance
with Syria. Although there may be some suspicions in Tehran as to the
kind of terms that Syria is actually willing to accept for a settlement, the
more general expectation is that the negotiations will falter or be blocked
for other reasons, including Israeli obduracy or other developments in the
area. Current Iranian policy thus appears to be based on delaying the
moment of truth regarding Syria's position on a settlement and future
relations with Damascus as long as possible, hoping that no crucial
decisions in this regard will eventually have to be made. But Iran's
options seem strictly limited anyway. To sever ties with Damascus
would only aggravate the generally pessimistic prognosis of the Qom
report and would not alleviate Iran's central concerns regarding increased regional isolation and a growing tide of anti-Iranian, anti-Islamic
sentiment. The choices of a substitute partnership or alliance to replace
that with Syria also appear severely restricted: no other force or local
power can support Iran across the whole spectrum of its political and
strategic interests, despite openings to Iraq, Egypt or other Arab parties.
The bottom line for Iran is that a severance of ties with Syria would
seriously jeopardize both the balance with Iraq and the chances of
continued access to Lebanon and its Shiite base – an outcome that few in
Tehran are likely to regard with equanimity.

The alliance with Iran does not appear to have been debated publicly
and openly within Syria's various political fora. The close control over
foreign policy maintained by President Assad and his inner circle should
not, however, be taken to imply that the relationship with Iran arouses no
internal dissent or dissatisfaction. Several loci of opposition to the relationship with Iran can be identified, including both secular and religious
elements. On the ultra-religious side, the remnants of the Ikhwan and
their associates are unlikely to have forgotten their failed appeal to
Tehran to come out in public against the regime during the internal
struggle of the early 1980s. The more traditional Sunni elite is also likely
to be suspicious of an alliance with an activist Shiite regime that may
perpetuate the current political status quo in favour of the Alawites.
Moderates within the Syrian leadership find little common ground with
Iranian 'extremism' and will be embarrassed by the association with
Iran, particularly at a time when Syrian interests lie in developing its

relations with the West and eradicating its past 'radical' image. Among senior Baath party officials, both secular and religious, opposition to the alliance stems from the Arab nationalist ideological roots of the party and its opposition to Persian/Shiite aggrandizement or the substitution for pan-Arab alignments of an alliance with a non-Arab, non-secular party. Similar feelings towards Iran may be registered by Christian elements within the party and state institutions who feel threatened by the overtly Islamic content of Iranian rhetoric and its possible erosion of Syria's long-standing secular Arab political tradition. Finally, elements within the military and security forces are concerned about Iran's role in Lebanon and the possibility that Iranian 'mischief', via Hizbullah, for instance, could precipitate an unwanted confrontation with Israel or even spiral out of control within Syria itself.

Chapter 7

Conclusion: a limited alliance

An alliance of limited costs and liabilities

From the Syrian perspective, the continuing alliance with Iran has served a number of vital interests by providing the following:

- a counterbalance to Iraq and a means of leverage against it;
- a regional strategic counterbalance to Israel;
- a means of containment and influence among the Shiite community in Lebanon;
- influence and leverage in the Gulf;
- influence among radical and Islamic groups in Lebanon/Palestine and elsewhere in the Middle East;
- a means of influence and engagement with the West;
- a source of military cooperation and economic support;
- a means of containing Islamic radical opposition within Syria itself.

From the Iranian point of view, the alliance with Syria has provided:

- a means of leverage against Iraq;
- access to the Shia community in Lebanon;
- access to the arena of the Arab–Israeli conflict, thus enhancing Iran's regional role;
- a major Arab partner, thus mitigating the chances of Arab–Persian polarization in the area;
- a means of reducing Sunni–Shia polarization in the Arab and Islamic arenas;
- an intermediary with the other Arab states, particularly in the Gulf;
- a means of reducing Iran's international isolation;
- a source of military support and an economic and trading partner.

117

Conclusion

For both Syria and Iran the overall cost of maintaining their alliance has been minimal since its inception. In essence, both sides have seen their alliance in defensive terms: more as a reaction to presumed hostile intent on the part of other regional or extra-regional powers than as a basis for joint positive action for the attainment of clearly defined common goals. In this sense, the Arab–Israeli peace process has not impinged on the relationship in any evident manner since 1991. Equally, judging from the evidence so far, it appears that the alliance will affect the process only in so far as it is seen by *both* parties as a common threat. If at any particular stage developments related to the peace process appear as a threat to *one* of the two sides then the other side will most likely react in accordance with its own percieved national interests. Such a threat perception, however, is more likely to be Iranian than Syrian. Since the Madrid conference of 1991 Syria has become progressively more committed to the peace process and a total reversal of its policy has become an increasingly remote possibility, barring any major change in the regime or the departure of the current Syrian leadership. Despite the slow pace of its negotiations with Israel and its criticisms of both the separate Palestinian and Jordanian deals, Syria's threat perceptions centre less on a continuation of the peace process than on the possibility of its breakdown. In other words, Syria now sees the successful culmination of the process on its (and Lebanon's) bilateral track with Israel as a necessary condition of protecting its own national interests – but not at any price.

More generally, the Syrian–Iranian alliance has had little effect on the ability of either party to pursue its independent national interests and objectives, even where these have not been shared by the other partner. In this sense, the alliance does not appear to have persisted at the expense of either Syrian or Iranian local, Arab or international policies. A quick review of major Syrian positions since the early 1980s substantiates this view. During this period, Syria:

- stood against the Iranian occupation of Iraqi soil in the Iraq-Iran war after 1982, and joined other Arab parties in condemning Iran's pursuit of the war against Iraq;
- actively cooperated politically and militarily with the United States in Operation Desert Storm and in allowing for the large-scale deployment of Western forces to the Gulf area;
- joined the Damascus Declaration, which excluded Iran but gave Syria itself (a non-Gulf power) a Gulf role;
- consistently supported the Arab-Gulf stance on Abu Musa and the Tunbs against the official Iranian line;

- joined the Madrid peace process in direct partnership with the United States under the banner of US 'even-handedness' regarding the Middle East peace process;
- maintained its control over Hizbullah in South Lebanon and engineered where necessary indirect agreements with Israel regarding Hizbullah activities (such as the July 1993 South Lebanon understanding concerning attacks on civilians);
- maintained close relations with Egypt and Saudi Arabia with a view to creating a new tripartite Arab bloc;
- maintained a continuous and multilevel political and diplomatic dialogue with the United States.

For its part, Iran:

- was not deterred from seeking arms from Israel during the war with Iraq;
- was not deterred from pursuing this war into Iraqi territory after 1982, despite Syrian objections;
- maintained links with Iraq, including an effective detente with Saddam, despite the two Gulf wars;
- was not deterred from its hard line in the Gulf regarding Abu Musa and the Tunbs;
- maintained its role and agenda in Lebanon (while accepting Syrian dominance within limits).

The durability of the Syrian–Iranian relationship despite such apparently incompatible policies can be partly explained by the very disparate nature of the regimes themselves and hence, somewhat paradoxically, by their high degree of tolerance for each other. For Iran, Syria remains by and large a non-Islamic regime which cannot be expected to behave according to the ideological strictures of the Islamic Republic itself. Tehran acknowledges the secular basis of Baathism and the hard-headed pragmatism that characterizes much of Syrian policy. By the same token, Syria recognizes the unique nature and aspirations of the political and clerical establishments in Tehran and does not expect Iran to abide by the same rules of behaviour that govern other Middle Eastern states. Each side thus tends not to be surprised, disappointed or unduly concerned by actions by the other party that would superficially appear to be inconsistent with its own beliefs and political precepts. The ability to accommodate the other side thus stems from the mutual recognition that neither seeks to emulate the other or to compete with it on its own terms. The net result is a surprisingly stable relationship reinforced by a realistic assessment of the limitations of the alliance and the common objectives it is able to serve.

An alliance of peripheral conflicting interests

This mutual tolerance is also highlighted and sustained by the very different set of national priorities of each side. In broad terms, Iran's current and projected short- to medium-term list of strategic concerns look something like this:

- developing the national economy and sustaining acceptable levels of economic performance and growth;
- maintaining internal sectarian and ethnic cohesion and stability, and guarding against ethnic disintegration; managing tensions such as those with the Kurds and the Sunni minority;
- addressing issues of financial solvency and managing the price and export of oil;
- stabilizing the Iranian 'northern tier', including relations with Turkey, Russia, Azerbaijan and the Central Asian republics;
- preserving and developing Iran's military capabilities;
- stabilizing relations with Iraq and maintaining vigilance regarding the Iraqi regime;
- stabilizing the conflict in Afghanistan and maintaining good relations with India and Pakistan;
- addressing Gulf concerns, including the Western military presence, relations with Saudi Arabia and management of the dispute with Abu Dhabi over Abu Musa and the Tunbs;
- managing relations with the West and particularly the United States, including the perceived US-led political and diplomatic offensive against Iran;
- exercising a role in the Arab–Israeli arena, with regard to Lebanon, the peace process and the potential for escalating tensions with Israel;
- pursuing its own broader political and ideological concerns in the Islamic, Arab and international arenas.

By way of contrast, Syria's list of strategic concerns can be prioritized as follows:

- ensuring internal political stability and the continuity of the regime;
- managing the peace process with Israel and pursuing Syria's objectives in a settlement;
- stabilizing the situation in Lebanon, and maintaining Syrian influence and control in the Lebanese arena;
- developing its economy;
- maintaining its defence capabilities and its minimal deterrent against Israel;
- consolidating the emerging relationship with the United States and the development of Syrian–US ties;
- strengthening its Arab and Gulf role through the maintenance and development of relations with Egypt and Saudi Arabia;
- maintaining vigilance regarding Iraq and the prospects of the Saddam regime;
- managing relations with Turkey and Iran, including the Kurds (trilateral), 'Islamic fundamentalism' (bilateral with Iran), the water issue (bilateral with Turkey), etc.;
- monitoring and managing developments within its immediate Arab zones of interest, e.g. Jordan and the Palestinians.

Syria's alliance with Iran has created a broad linkage between Arab–Israeli and Gulf issues for both partners. So far at least, the alliance has had no evident effect either on Syrian policy towards an Arab–Israeli settlement or on Iranian policy towards the Gulf. What the alliance therefore appears to comprise is a tacit or otherwise undeclared understanding on a fundamental trade-off between the vital interests of both sides: a relative free hand for Syria in dealing with Arab–Israeli issues and the question of a negotiated settlement with Israel in return for a relatively free hand for Iran in dealing with its Gulf interests and objectives. Syrian toleration of Iran's Gulf policies is thus partly reflected in the tone of Iran's positions on Syria's participation in the peace process: Iran's Gulf 'intransigence' is coupled with a relatively conciliatory and understanding position regarding Syria and the Arab–Israeli conflict.

Within this context common Syrian–Iranian priorities can be seen to be largely peripheral to either side's central strategic concerns. As such the potential for a serious conflict of interests between the two is minimized and the incentive to maintain the relationship is reinforced. Iran thus broadly accepts Syria's freedom of action and management of issues pertaining to Israel, Lebanon, the United States and the peace process, while Syria broadly accepts Iran's dealings with Iraq and the Gulf, and its links with 'fundamentalism' (including the Shia of Lebanon). Israel represents a dominant concern for Syria but is of relatively secondary salience for Iran: Iran accordingly concedes Syria's right to deal with the Israeli issue as it sees fit. Conversely, Syria acknowledges the salience of Gulf issues for Iran and accords Iran considerable leeway in managing such issues as it sees fit. Where the interests of both sides converge, such as over Iraq, neither side is likely to undertake any radical steps in challenging the minimum agreed basis of their common approach.

Select bibliography

Abrahamian, E., 1993. *Khomeinism: Essays on the Iranian Republic*, London: I.B. Tauris.

AbuKhalil, A., 1990. 'Syria and the Shiites: Al-Asad's Policy in Lebanon', *Third World Quarterly*, 12: 2, April.

Ammar, N., 1994. 'Palestinian–Iranian Relations: Origins, Conflicts and Collapse', unpublished paper [in Arabic], Tunis.

Bakash, S., 1990. 'Iran's Relations with Israel, Syria and Lebanon', in M. Rezun (ed.), *Iran at the Crossroads: Global Relations in a Turbulent Decade*, Boulder, CO: Westview.

Calabrese, J., 1990. 'Iran II: The Damascus Connection', *The World Today*, 46: 10, October.

Caret, C., 1987. '"L'alliance contre-nature" de la Syrie baasiste et de la République islamique d'Iran', *Politique Etrangère*, 52: 2.

Chubin, S., 1994. *Iran's National Security Policy: Capabilities, Intentions and Impact*, Washington, DC: Carnegie Endowment for International Peace.

Clawson, P., 1993. *Iran's Challenge to the West: How, When and Why?*, Washington, DC: Policy Paper no. 33, Washington Institute for Near East Policy.

Davis, Z., and Donnelly, W., 1993. *Iran's Nuclear Activities and the Congressional Response*, Washington, DC: CRS Issues Brief, Library of Congress, 28 March.

Deeb, M., 1988. 'Shia Movements in Lebanon: Their Formation, Ideology, Social Basis and Links with Iran and Syria', *Third World Quarterly*, 10: 2, April.

Diab, Z., 1994. 'Have Syria and Israel Opted for Peace?', *Middle East Policy*, 3: 2, July.

Drysdale, A., and Hinnebusch, R., 1991. *Syria and the Middle East Peace Process*, New York: Council on Foreign Relations.

Ehteshami, A., 1993. 'The Armed Forces of the Islamic Republic of Iran', *Jane's Intelligence Review*, February.

Select bibliography

——, 1992. 'Iranian Rearmament Strategy under President Rafsanjani', *Jane's Intelligence Review*, July.

Eisenstadt, M., 1993. 'Syria's Strategic Weapons', *Jane's Intelligence Review*, April.

——, 1992. *Arming for Peace? Syria's Elusive Quest for 'Strategic Parity'*, Washington, DC: Policy Paper no. 31, Washington Institute for Near East Policy.

Fuller, G.E., 1991. *The Center of the Universe: The Geopolitics of Iran*, Boulder, CO: Westview (a RAND Corporation study).

Goodarzi, Jubin, 1990. 'The Pragmatic Entente: Syrian–Iranian Relations 1979–1989', Washington, DC, unpublished paper, February.

Hamzeh, Nizar A., 1993. 'Lebanon's Hizbullah: From Islamic Revolution to Parliamentary Accommodation', *Third World Quarterly*, 14: 2, April.

Hardesty, S., 1993. 'Iran, the Peace Process – and Syria', *US–Iran Review*, 1: 7, October.

Hashim, A., 1992. 'Resurgent Iran: New Defence Thinking and Growing Military Capabilities', unpublished paper.

Hirschfeld, Y., 1986. 'The Odd Couple: Baathist Syria and Khomeini's Iran', in M. Maoz and A. Yaniv (eds), *Syria Under Assad: Domestic Constraints and Regional Risks*, London: Croom Helm; Gustav Heinemann Institute of Middle Eastern Studies, University of Haifa.

Hitti, N., 1993. 'Lebanon in Iran's Foreign Policy: Opportunities and Constraints', in H. Amirahmadi and N. Entessar (eds), *Iran and the Arab World*, London: Macmillan.

Hunter, S., 1993. 'Iran and Syria: From Hostility to Limited Alliance', in H. Amirahmadi and N. Entessar (eds), *Iran and the Arab World*, London: Macmillan.

——, 1990. 'Iran and the Arab World', in M. Rezun (ed.), *Iran at the Crossroads: Global Relations in a Turbulent Decade*, Boulder, CO: Westview.

——, 1985. 'Syrian–Iranian Relations: An Alliance of Convenience or More?', *Middle East Insight*, 4: 2, June/July.

Katzman, K., 1993. *Current Developments and US Policy*, Washington, DC: CRS Issues Brief, Library of Congress, 27 May.

Kazemi, F., 1985. 'Iran, Israel and the Arab–Israeli Balance', in B. Rosen (ed.), *Iran since the Revolution*, New York: Social Science Monographs, Columbia University Press.

Kemp, G., 1994. *Forever Enemies? American Policy and the Islamic Republic of Iran*, Washington, DC: Carnegie Endowment.

Khalidi, A.S., and Agha, H., 1991. 'The Syrian Doctrine of Strategic Parity', in J. Kipper and H. Saunders (eds), *The Middle East in Global Perspective*, Boulder, CO: Westview.

Kienle, E., 1990. *Ba'th v Ba'th: The Conflict between Syria and Iraq 1968–1989*, London: I.B. Tauris.

Kodmani-Darwish, B., 1994. 'Syrie: anciens dilemmes, nouvelles stratégies', in B. Kodmani-Darwish and M. Chartouny-Dubarry, *Perceptions de securité et stratégies nationales au moyen orient*, Paris: Institut Français des Relations Internationales.

Kramer, M., 1990. 'Redeeming Jerusalem: The Pan-Islamic Premise of Hizbullah', in D. Menshari (ed.), *The Iranian Revolution and the Muslim world*, Boulder, CO: Westview.

——, 1987. 'Syria's Alawis and Shi'ism', in M. Kramer (ed.), *Shi'ism, Resistance and Revolution*, Boulder, CO: Westview.

Mara'i, M., and Halabi, U., 1992. 'Life under Occupation in the Golan Heights', *Journal of Palestine Studies*, 12: 1, Autumn.

Marschall, C., 1991. 'Syria, Iran and the changing Middle East order: the Syro-Iranian alliance 1979–1988', unpublished M.Phil. thesis, Oxford University.

Muslih, M., 1993. 'The Golan: Israel, Syria and Strategic Calculations', *Middle East Journal*, 47: 4, Autumn.

Olmert, Y., 1994. *Toward a Syrian–Israeli Peace Agreement: Perspective of a Former Negotiator*, Washington, DC: Research Memorandum no. 25, Washington Institute for Near East Policy, April.

——, 1990. 'Iranian–Syrian Relations', in D. Menshari (ed.), *The Iranian Revolution and the Muslim world*, Boulder CO: Westview.

Pipes, D., 1991. *Damascus Courts the West: Syrian Politics, 1989–1991*, Washington, DC: Policy Papers no. 26, Washington Institute for Near East Policy.

Quandt, W., 1993. *Peace Process: American Diplomacy and the Arab–Israeli Conflict since 1967*, Berkeley, CA, and Washington DC: University of California Press/The Brookings Institution.

Ramazani, R.K., 1988. *Revolutionary Iran: Challenge and Response in the Middle East*, Baltimore and London: Johns Hopkins University Press.

Rosen, B. (ed.), 1985. *Iran since the Revolution*, New York: Social Science Monographs, Columbia University Press.

Roy, O., 1993. *The Failure of Political Islam*, London: I.B. Tauris.

Saphir, Y., 1994. 'Proliferation of Non-conventional Weapons in the Middle East', in S. Gazit (ed.), *The Middle East Military Balance*, Tel Aviv: Jaffe Centre for Strategic Studies.

Sariolghlam, M., 1993. 'Conceptual Sources of Post-Revolutionary Iranian Behaviour toward the Arab World', in J. Amirahmadi and N. Entessar (eds), *Iran and the Arab World*, London: Macmillan.

Seale, P., 1988. *Asad of Syria: The Struggle for the Middle East*, London: I.B. Tauris.

Sobhani, S., 1989. *The Pragmatic Entente: Israeli–Iranian Relations 1948–1988*, New York: Praeger.

Sukkar, N., 1994. 'The Crisis of 1986', in E. Kienle (ed.), *Contemporary Syria: Liberalization between Cold War and Cold Peace*, London: British Academic Press.

Select bibliography

Vaziri, H., 1992. 'Iran's Involvement in Lebanon: Polarization and Radicalization of Militant Islamic Movements', *Journal of South Asian and Middle Eastern Studies*, 16: 2, Winter.

Wright, R., 1988. 'Lebanon', in S. Hunter (ed.), *The Politics of Islamic Revivalism*, Bloomington and Indianapolis: Indiana University Press.

also in this series ...

edited by
Peter Ferdinand

THE NEW CENTRAL ASIA AND ITS NEIGHBOURS

128 pages; 216x138mm
ISBN 1 85567 139 5 (pbk)

In Central Asia hope and anxiety have alternated since the collapse of the Soviet Union. On the one hand, its peoples are now closer to being masters of their destiny than at any time this century. On the other hand the civil war in Tajikistan is a constant reminder of the fragility of ethnic and clan relations in the region as a whole. Meanwhile, other states, especially neighbouring ones, look on nervously.

This study focuses both on developments inside the five republics – Kazakhstan, Kyrgyzstan, Tajikistan, Turkmenistan and Uzbekistan – and on their relations with neighbouring states. It pays particular attention to the development of economic cooperation in the region. It starts by examining the republics' history and the extent to which they had a Central Asian identity in the past and are trying to create one now. Further chapters deal with relations with Russia, including the official policies of the republics, and popular attitudes towards their Russian minorities; relations with the Middle East, in particular Iran, Turkey and Israel; the impact on South Asia, particularly the rivalry between India and Pakistan (including over Kashmir), and the interaction with the civil war in Afghanistan; and the impact on China,especially on Xinjiang and the more general relationship between the centre and the provinces.

Dr Peter Ferdinand is Director of the Centre for Studies in Democratization at the University of Warwick and was formerly the Head of the Asia-Pacific Programme at the Royal Institute of International Affairs.

October 1994 · RIIA/Pinter   Price £9.99

Chatham House
Papers

 THE ROYAL INSTITUTE OF
INTERNATIONAL AFFAIRS

forthcoming in this series ...

Michael Cox

US FOREIGN POLICY AFTER THE COLD WAR
Superpower Without a Mission?

The United States triumphed in the Cold War but has since found it extraordinarily difficult to define a clear international mission for itself. As a result the euphoria of an earlier period – which reached its climax in 1991 with US victory in the Gulf war and the collapse of the USSR – has given way to confusion about America's proper purpose in the 'new world order'.

In this wide-ranging study, the author seeks to understand the dilemmas and problems facing the United States in the world today through a detailed examination of six large issues: the domestic constraints facing US foreign policy-makers after the Cold War; the new geoeconomic imperative that is redefining the very character of the national security debate; the continued centrality of the Russian question in American global calculations; the diminishing but still crucial role of American military power; US dilemmas in the new Europe; and whether or not the United States is turning away from Europe towards the Pacific Rim.

The book concludes with a discussion of two controversial questions. Whatever happened to the Third World – the epicentre of the Cold War for nearly thirty years? And what are the chances of American foreign policy ever regaining the clarity it had in an earlier epoch?

Michael Cox is Reader in Politics at the Queen's University of Belfast, and Associate Fellow at the Royal Institute of International Affairs.

144 pages; 216x138mm
ISBN 1 85567 221 9 (pbk)

autumn 1995   RIIA/Pinter   Price £9.99

Chatham House Papers

THE ROYAL INSTITUTE OF
INTERNATIONAL AFFAIRS

forthcoming in this series ...

Joseph Kostiner

YEMEN
The Fluctuations of Unity

This study examines the unification process between
North and South Yemen, from the preparations during the 1970s and 1980s which preceded union in
1990, through its subsequent evolution and the problems that led to internal war and the occupation of
South Yemen by North Yemeni forces in 1994, con-
cluding with some thoughts on the implications of
this forced unity.

Within the broad context of post-Cold War conditions,
the Gulf war and inter-Arab relations, Yemeni hopes
for unification are examined, as are the reasons why
these were to be frustrated, with the coexistence of
two rival state systems and communities. Attention
is paid to the role of Islamic and tribal groups and
values, and special emphasis is placed on the
convulsions accompanying democratization.

Dr Joseph Kostiner is at the Moshe Dayan Centre
for Middle Eastern and African Studies, Tel Aviv
University, Israel.

Readership
Middle East specialists
social scientists
policy analysts
policy-makers

128 pages; 216x138mm
ISBN 1 85567 348 7 (pbk)

January 1996   RIIA/Pinter   Price £10.99